SAILING THE FOREST

SAILING THE FOREST

SELECTED POEMS

ROBIN ROBERTSON

FARRAR, STRAUS AND GIROUX   NEW YORK

Farrar, Straus and Giroux
18 West 18th Street, New York 10011

Library of Congress Cataloging-in-Publication Data
Robertson, Robin, 1955–
    [Poems. Selections]
    Sailing the forest : selected poems / Robin Robertson.
      pages   cm
    ISBN 978-0-374-25534-3 (hardback)
    I. Title.

PR6068.O1925A6 2014
821'.914—dc23

                                        2014031271

Farrar, Straus and Giroux books may be purchased for educational, business,
or promotional use. For information on bulk purchases, please contact the
Macmillan Corporate and Premium Sales Department at 1-800-221-7945,
extension 5442, or write to specialmarkets@macmillan.com.

www.fsgbooks.com
www.twitter.com/fsgbooks • www.facebook.com/fsgbooks

1 3 5 7 9 10 8 6 4 2

The flowers of the forest they ask it of me,
How many strawberries grow in the salt sea?
And I answered to them with a tear in my eye,
How many dark ships sail the forest?

Contents

SAILING THE FOREST

NEW GRAVITY

Treading through the half-light of ivy
and headstone, I see you in the distance
as I'm telling our daughter
about this place, this whole business:
a sister about to be born,
how a life's new gravity suspends in water.
Under the oak, the fallen leaves
are pieces of the tree's jigsaw;
by your father's grave you are pressing acorns
into the shadows to seed.

THREE WAYS OF LOOKING AT GOD

1.

A claustrophobia of sand and stone: a walled heat.
The light bleaches and curves like a blade, isolates
the chirr of crickets, seed-pods detonating,
the valley waiting in a film of flame.
A bird finds an open channel in the air
and follows it without exertion to the branch.

2.

The sky is slashed like a sail. Night folds
over the shears, the dye, the docked tails.
We listen to the rumours of the valley:
goats' voices, gear-changes, the stirring of dogs.
In the green light, lambs with rouged cheeks
skitter from their first communion, calling for home.

3.

Lightning flexes: a man chalked on a board, reeling,
exact, elementary, flawed; at each kick, birds flinch
and scatter from the white lawn.
The long trees bend to the grain of the gale,
streaming the dark valley like riverweed.
All night: thunder, torn leaves; a sheathing of wings.

ADVENT IN CO. FERMANAGH

Two chemists in one village,
side by side,
ours and theirs;
both specialise in cattle cures.
The greengrocer, meanwhile,
doubles as undertaker;
his potatoes
always hard and white,
beautifully laid out.

The town is bottle-shaped
and dressed for Christmas
in a morse code of coloured lights,
marginal snow
in crescents at the windows,
and on the sill,
in the holly's gloss
of red and starred green,
illuminating angels.

Leaning men on corners watch
the circumspect, the continent,
linking their way to church.
Then the mid-day angelus
opens the doors in the street
like organ stops,
for the pinched and raddled
in their penitential suits
pulling children out of doorways:
strings of hankies from a sleeve.

No one watches the soldiers
walking backwards on patrol:
the cellophane crackle of radios,
the call and answer
as they stroll, each cradling
a weapon like a newborn.

Stooped under hangovers,
the pasty supplicants
file towards the priest
to say 'Aaah' for atonement,
and shuffle out, cowed,
in a cold sweat,
His Body
tucked behind the teeth.

Doors disclose them,
scribbling down the hill
for rashers and egg
and wheaten bread;
Guinness and Black Bush:
gifts for the back room
with the curtains pulled.

Sunlight glints
like mica schist on granite
on the huddled homes
as the rain comes casting down.

Stone circles of sheep
in the drowned field
watch helicopters come
dreaming over hedges:
horse-flies the size of houses,
great machines
for opening the air,
and shaking it shut.
Leaving an absence, a silence,
and a hatch of light
which discovers a door.
The town drunk emerges
gingerly from the bar,
amazed by the familiar;
patting his pockets,
blinking like Lazarus.

STATIC

The storm shakes out its sheets
against the darkening window:
the glass flinches under thrown hail.
Unhinged, the television slips its hold,
streams into black and white
then silence, as the lines go down.
Her postcards stir on the shelf, tip over;
the lights of Calais trip out one by one.

He cannot tell her
how the geese scull back at twilight,
how the lighthouse walks its beam
across the trenches of the sea.
He cannot tell her how the open night
swings like a door without her,
how he is the lock
and she is the key.

SHEELA-NA-GIG

He has reached her island by stones
pegged in swollen water,
through rain that has fallen for days.

He touches the welling mouth, the split stone;
she shows him the opening folds
where rainwater troubles and turns.

The rain slows, and stops; light deepens
at the lid of the lake, the water creased
by the head of an otter, body of a bird.

THE FLAYING OF MARSYAS

after Ovid

I.

A bright clearing. Sun among the leaves,
sifting down to dapple the soft ground, and rest
a gilded bar against the muted flanks of trees.
In the flittering green light the glade
listens in and breathes.

A wooden pail; some pegs, a coil of wire;
a bundle of steel flensing knives.

Spreadeagled between two pines,
hooked at each hoof to the higher branches,
tied to the root by his hands, flagged
as his own white cross,
the satyr Marsyas hangs.

Three stand as honour guard:
two apprentices, one butcher.

II.

Let's have a look at you, then.
Bit scrawny for a satyr,
all skin and whipcord, is it?

Soon find out.
So, think you can turn up with your stag-bones
and out-play Lord Apollo?
This'll learn you. Fleece the fucker.
Sternum to groin.
Tickle does it? Fucking bastard,
coming down here with your dirty ways . . .
Armpit to wrist, both sides.
Chasing our women . . .
Fine cuts round hoof and hand and neck.
Can't even speak the language proper.
Transverse from umbilicus to iliac crest,
half-circling the waist.
Jesus. You fucking stink, you do.
Hock to groin, groin to hock.
That's your inside leg done:
no more rutting for you, cunt.

Now. One of you on each side.
Blade along the bone, find the tendon,
nick it and peel, nice and slow.
A bit of shirt-lifting, now, to purge him,
pull his wool over his eyes
and show him Lord Apollo's rapture;
pelt on one tree, him on another:
the inner man revealed.

III.

Red Marsyas. Marsyas *écorché*,
splayed, shucked of his skin
in a tug and rift of tissue;
his birthday suit sloughed
the way a sodden overcoat is eased
off the shoulders and dumped.
All memories of a carnal life
lifted like a bad tattoo,
live bark from the vascular tree:
raw Marsyas unsheathed.

Or dragged from his own wreckage,
dressed in red ropes
that plait and twine his trunk
and limbs into true definition,
he assumes the flexed pose of the hero:
the straps and buckles of ligament
glisten and tick on the sculpture
of Marsyas, muscle-man.
Mr Universe displays the map of his body:
the bulbs of high ground carved
by the curve of gully and canal,
the tributaries tight as ivy or the livid vine,
and everywhere, the purling flux of blood
in the land and the swirl of it flooding away.

Or this: the shambles of Marsyas.
The dark chest meat marbled with yellow fat,
his heart like an animal breathing

in its milky envelope,
the viscera a well-packed suitcase
of chitterlings, palpitating tripe.
A man dismantled, a tatterdemalion
torn to steak and rind,
a disappointing pentimento
or the toy that can't be re-assembled
by the boy Apollo, raptor, vivisector.

The sail of stretched skin thrills and snaps
in the same breeze that makes his nerves
fire, his bare lungs scream.
Stripped of himself and from his twin:
the stiffening scab and the sticky wound.

Marsyas the martyr, a god's fetish,
hangs from the tree like bad fruit.

ABERDEEN

The grey sea turns in its sleep
disturbing seagulls from the green rock.

We watched the long collapse, the black drop
and frothing of the toppled wave; looked out
on the dark that goes to Norway.

We lay all night in an open boat, that rocked
by the harbour wall – listening to the tyres creak
at the stone quay, trying to keep time –
till the night-fishers came in their arc, their lap
of light: the fat slap of waves, the water's
sway, the water mullioned with light.

The sifting rain, italic rain; the smirr
that drifted down for days; the sleet.
Your hair full of hail, as if sewn there.
In the damp sheets we left each other sea-gifts,
watermarks: long lost now in all these years
of the rip-tide's swell and trawl.

All night the feeding storm banked up
the streets and houses. In the morning
the sky was yellow, the frost ringing.

The grey sea turns in its sleep
disturbing seagulls from the green rock.

PIBROCH

Foam in the sand-lap of the north-sea water
fizzles out – leaves the beach mouthing –
the flecks of the last kiss
kissed away by the next wave, rushing;
each shearing over its own sea-valve
as it turns with a shock into sound.

And how I long now for the pibroch,
pibroch long and slow, lamenting all this:
all this longing for the right wave,
for the special wave that toils
behind the pilot but can never find a home –
find my edge to crash against,
my darkness for its darknesses
my hands amongst its foam.

FIREWORKS

'In the greatness of the flame he gave up the ghost'
Foxe's Book of Martyrs, XI

The poplars are emptied at dusk
like blown matches. A gust frees
and scatters the leaves in their last blaze:
the bronze husks catch and cartwheel
round and down the street to the park
in the smoke of a dark autumn,
from the thin, extinguished trees.

In the small lake, what had once been water
now was seamed with smoke,
marbled and macular,
dim and deep as wax,
with each stick and twig like a spilled wick
in the dulling hollow of the sconce:
metamorphosis in the cancelled pond.

By midnight the ice was dished, percussive,
blue-black under a bone moon.
Skipping stones on its steel deck
gave the sound of thrown springs,
railway lines, or fence-wire, singing.
I had scored a tracery of leaving, a map engraved,
a thrilling in the air.

After the park, the garden,
and the bright litter of the night's display:
a stubble of burnt-out cones and candles,
cold star-shells, burst and charred,
a catherine wheel fused to the bark;
scorched bottles, tapers; smoke, hanging;
the softening box on its bed of ash.

Hands cupped around a match's flame:
the blue twist of smoke. Petrol
is the fifth element: opening
a door in the night I can leave through.
Across the city, a scratch of light
disappears. I hear its stick
clattering in the trees.

JACK-IN-THE-GREEN

Grinning soldiers
patrolling the border with biscuits,

tricked out in a motley of green and grey,
sooty faces, and leaves
where their hair should have been.

We came across one in the garden,
crouching: the Green Man abroad,
a compost of flesh and grass and metal,

haunched like a dog caught
shivering at its stool.

HANDS OF A FARMER IN CO. TYRONE

He wore fish-gutter's gloves to pick brambles:
scoured leather, without fingertips,
so his fist could find the insides of the bush
and open around the soft black heart,
for the easing of the fruit.
He was a thorn in the fenced garden:
his hand at the command wire
paying out the line from culvert to sheugh.
They were on his land,
so he pulled the road up by the root.

MOVING HOUSE

I. MIDDLE WATCH, BATTERSEA

Wash of traffic: the crush
of waves on a windowed shore;

the windows, worn to a shiver, let in rain.
The wind is posting litter through the door.

Behind the gas-fire in the hearth
a soot-fall clears the chimney's throat

and the wind sings wire-songs: the element
blown like coal to a white gasp.

A scuffle in the skirting-board
as something frees itself from something else.

The bulb stirs and the room shifts
twice towards the cellar door.

II. DEFROSTING

The satisfying creak and give
of another white slab: ridged,
tectonic, holding the ice-box shape
in a curved mould; as if the polystyrene
once packed around the fridge
now packed inside, heavier and cold.
Small ice clatters in the salad drawer
as I hack at the top with a knife,
hands raw and hot in the sharp snow.
Bored, I take a warm beer through and write.
The fridge ticks with water, dripping;
the kitchen bobs towards me in the night.

ARTICHOKE

The nubbed leaves
come away
in a tease of green, thinning
down to the membrane:
the quick, purpled,
beginnings of the male.

Then the slow hairs of the heart:
the choke that guards its trophy,
its vegetable goblet.
The meat of it lies, displayed,
up-ended, *al dente*,
the stub-root aching in its oil.

SILVER LAKE, VERMONT

Familiar gestures in a fresh hand:
the lint and balsam,
sanctuary of the cooled flesh.
Under a tissue moon, your hair untied,
your hair held back, the balm
of chrism dribbed against your side.

THE IMMORALIST

In the sleeping ward, night-nurses
gather at my curtained bed,
looming like Rembrandts, drawing
their winged heads in around
the surgeon at my side.
The golden section lit by anglepoise:
the wrinkled fruit, some books,
my chest strapped like a girl's
to stem the leaking wound.

Scissoring the grey crêpe
released a clot dark as liver:
an African plum in its syrup
slid into my lap.
Jesus, I said, as the doctor called for swabs,
more light, the stitching trolley.
Without anaesthetics he worked quickly,
his pale hands deft
as a guitarist at the frets.
This is what they'd been waiting for:
one hand at the pliant flesh,
the other subduing it with suture
and a blurred knot.
Five minutes and it was over,
and he was smiling at the Gide
amongst the magazines and grapes:
Used to be just TB, this place, he said,
my blood on his cheek like a blush.

As the nurse drew back the curtain, she warned:
There will be pain.
Night flooded, streaming slowly into shape;
I heard the tinnitus of radio,
saw the humped figure under his lung of light,
the earphones' plastic stirrup on its hook,
his left hand in place on the white bandage
his right hand holding my book.

SHOT

You sleep as I stumble
room to room, unhelmed,
heavy-greaved;
coming to you
through gorse-light
and the fallen trees:
heraldic, blessed
with wounds.
Red-handed at the key
I was stock-still, gazing back
at deer-slots in the snow:
flushed, quick from the kill,
carrying my shot,
my sadness like a stone.
In the quarry-hole of your bed
you're sleeping still.

THE FLOWERS OF THE FOREST

Shouldering my daughter
like a set of pipes
I walk her
to a dead march
and counterpoint her crying
with my hummed drone:
the floo'ers o' the forest
are a' wi'ed awae

my cracked reed
blanking
on the high note,
the way a nib runs dry
in the rut it makes,
and splays.

SIX VIEWS FROM THE CAMERA OBSCURA

You are in another country, I know, but I did
just see you on that corner, clearly,
then passing in that cab, head down,
dashing me a note perhaps. The sap of you
still on my hands. A trace.
Wait. Wait for me here.

＊

The lens loses you in a blaze of traffic,
the murk of wynds; I track to the mouth
of Riddle's Court, to Lady Stair's Close,
but it clouds and I cannot find you. A clutch
of backpackers blocks my view, then the sun opens
and you are there. Your hair, your hand. A touch.

＊

Dawn: the harbour's curve
of stone – the shirr
of wind-flaw on water,
the falling of birds,
a woman waving
once from a window.

*

Both hands to her hair,
to the back of her head and the nape
of the neck, adjusting or unloosening
the warm braid in its simple knot;
the hair damp and heavy in her hands,
the root of each arm laid open and bare.

*

In the Grassmarket, a girl in a red dress
steps between parked cars
into the forensic flash, flash of cameras.
Around her, the Pre-Raphaelite beauties
of Julia Margaret Cameron,
the mongols of Arbus.

*

What I thought was a figure
standing in a doorway
was just a doorway;
the movement in the window
just a loss of light. Look:
my eyes are not my own.

APART

We are drawn to edges, to our own
parapets and sea-walls: finding our lives
in relief, in some forked storm.

Returning with our unimaginable gifts,
badged with salt and blood,
we have forgotten how to walk.

Thinking how much more we wanted
when what we had was all there was;

looking too late to the ones we loved,
we stretch out our hands as we fall.

WEDDING THE LOCKSMITH'S DAUGHTER

The slow-grained slide to embed the blade
of the key is a sheathing,
a gliding on graphite, pushing inside
to find the ribs of the lock.

Sunk home, the true key slots to its matrix;
geared, tight-fitting, they turn
together, shooting the spring-lock,
throwing the bolt. Dactyls, iambics –

the clinch of words – the hidden couplings
in the cased machine. A chime of sound
on sound: the way the sung note snibs on meaning

and holds. The lines engage and marry now,
their bells are keeping time;
the church doors close and open underground.

THE LANGUAGE OF BIRDS

The sides of the hill
are stubbed with fire-pits.
The sky is paraffin blue.

A pigeon's heart swings here
on the kissing-gate, withered,
stuck through with pins,

while out on the estuary,
beaks of birds needle
to the wind's compass,

the sky's protocol.
Swans go singing out to sea,
the weather is changing cold.

*

In the elm above me, a magpie chuckles
and turns the magic wand of itself
away, towards the light.

I climb to the seeing rock
high over the pines; a blown squall
of rooks rises and settles like ash.

I saw the hay marry the fire
and the fire walk.
The sky went the colour of stone.

The cattle sickened:
what milk that came
came threaded, red as dawn.

*

Down below, in the grey fall
of heather and gorse,
a swithering flame.

Hooded crows haunt the highway,
pulling at roadkill;
their heads swivel to watch.

I've seen them murder their own,
the weak or the rare, those
with the gift of tongues.

I keep an albino one in a box.
I can't let go of it
till it tells me its name.

MAROON, OVER BLACK ON RED

THRESHOLD

In the fall of '58
at the Whitney,
trying to escape
a hated critic,
he missed the doorway
and put both hands
through the plate glass:
an after-image
of the black grave,
forecast in red.

MAROON

This is the light
through closed eyes:
the dark corona
fraying the edges
of the slammed door;
turbulence playing
in the face of it all –
the black ingots made
from absence, the red
drawn from life.

ART LESSON

She stood at his
burnt windows
until she saw herself
answered in their dark,
the way glass gets
blacked at night
in a lighted room.
She went home,
pulled the curtains;
drew a red bath.

EXIT

On the wall of the studio
on East 69th
his last canvas: a large,
unfinished study in reds.
On the floor: exsanguination
via the brachial artery;
six foot by eight;
black on red; unframed.
Signed by the artist
in the crook of his arm.

MARCH, LEWISBORO

for Shelby White & Leon Levy

The estate at dawn hangs
like smoke; the forest

drawn in grainy bands
of smeared, cross-hatched,

illegible trees: a botched
photocopy of itself.

Swamp maple, sugar maple,
red and white oak; first light lifts

the pale yellow flare
of a beech tree's papery leaves.

Where are you going?
What on earth's the time?

A salting of snow, blown
across the white table of the lake:

thrown leaves scrape and scratch
the hard new surface,

to be fluked away,
in another gust, like cards.

What life there is is felt and phantom:
limbs lost under the locking ice,

glimpsed, half-heard beginnings;
the vestiges, and signs.

Turn off the light! Please,
I'm trying to get some sleep.

The oiled rook strides
into the wind's current,

ransacks some twigs, then
opens herself into the air;

ducks, flummoxed, slither
and skite on the ice.

Run me a bath when you get back,
I'm freezing here.

The love-blind swan climbs out,
head crooked, neck folded flat,

to drag-walk and
swagger after the Canada goose.

His mate nests on the island;
will watch all this for months.

What's wrong with you
that you can never sleep?

In the sky, five crows
are bringing down a hawk –

their cries are lost
and he is lost,

among the pines, far out
over the reservoir.

The frost's acoustic
futile against such silence:

a dog's bark, like a gun,
just ricochets.

And if you're going to the store
you better get me my magazine.

Stations of the necessary dead:
the drenched mop of rabbit,

its eyes (which would have dimmed
like the drying of ink) not present;

the crow's umbrella spokes
abandoned in a pool of stress.

The soil's peristalsis
gives up baseballs, glass bottles,

its usual spoil of stone
eased to the surface

only to be erased again
by another fall;

the slub in the immaculate lawn
is the missing roe deer,

her warm wounds hung
in their sheaths of snow.

Why don't you come back to bed?
You can walk any time.

Wind breathes life into leaves
till the trees are speaking,

and under a sudden, exorbitant
flush of light,

a spruce stands
thickly green and lucent

over tiny arrows in the snow
pointing, unmistakably, to the junco

and the chickadee, flickers,
grosbeaks, a white-winged crossbill –

the feeder is ribboned with goldfinches,
sapsuckers: a maypole of birds.

Squirrels bicker underneath
in the spill of millet.

Do what you want.
You always do anyway.

On the slopes, daffodils begin to show
the green of their bills;

flower varieties, painted on sticks,
people the hollows:

Manon Lescaut is here,
and Jules Verne,

Rip Van Winkle bedded down
with Salome and Rosy Splendour;

Burning Heart, Martinette,
Gigantic Star.

And check the mail!
I'm expecting a letter.

Behind the house, stone sphinxes
and a line of statues, trussed up,

black-bagged for the frost:
like hostages

or the already cold and
unnegotiable dead.

Have you gone already?
I was talking to you.

White-tails have leapt an eight-foot fence
to crop the rhododendrons;

one by one
they raise their heads to stare

– stage-struck – then jink away,
amazed, back

into their element,
which is breath.

The sun has cleared the trees
but gives out

nothing now but glare.
All the colours are too bright:

the chemical red of a cardinal;
the forsythia's astringent

yellow gold; stars of glass
on the drive; all these radiant

cars and houses;
the speeding road.

My grey notebook.
This glossy magazine and mail.

BREAK

Washing glasses in the sink
and the first thing she knew was this
dull click, like a tongue,
under the soap-suds.
The foam pinked.
Now she could see blood
smoking from the flap of skin,
and it was over, clearly,
out in the open:
holding water, feeling nothing.

EXPOSURE

Rain, you said, *is silence turned up high.*
It has been raining now for days.
Even when it stops
there is still the sound
of rainwater, labouring
to find some way into the ground.

We lie in grim embrace: these
two halves trying to be whole, straining
for this break in the static,
in the white noise
that was rain falling
all day and all through the sheeted night.

Silence is rain with the sound turned down,
and I stare out now on a clear view
of something left out on the line:
a life, snagged there –
drenched, shrunken,
unrecognisably mine.

FALSE SPRING

A lift in the weather: a clemency
I cling to like the legend

of myself: self-exiled,
world-wounded, god

of evenings like this,
eighty degrees and half a world away.

⋆

All night, the industry
of erasure, effacement,

our one mouth
working itself dry.

⋆

But even a god can't stop the light
that finds us, annealed,

fruitless, two strangers
broken on the field of day.

In the window-box,
the narcissi come up blind.

DREAM OF THE HUNTRESS

It is always the same:
she is standing over me

in the forest clearing,
a dab of blood on her cheek

from a rabbit or a deer.
I am aware of nothing

but my mutinous flesh,
and the traps of desire

sent to test it –
her bare arms, bare

shoulders, her loosened hair,
the hard, high breasts,

and under a belt
of knives and fish-lures,

her undressed wound.
Every night the same:

the slashed fetlock,
the buckling under;

I wake in her body
broken, like a gun.

THE THERMAL IMAGE

The side of the house came away
like a glacier calving,
opening up four floors
in a suck of vertigo:
staircases walking nowhere,
doors going into the air –
the bedroom wallpaper
now clashing with the lawn,
the full-length mirror
mirroring the sky.

The shell is broken
and the building's heat is streaming out;
my camera sees it as a white cloud.
I pick up residuals from the wiring
and the hearth, faint glows
from a sofa and the fogged-up
roll-top bath. It's like cracking open
logs to find fireflies.

I move around the city
looking for the hotspots:
the heat signatures of love,
of too much blood;
one hundred watts at rest, rising
to a thousand *in extremis*.
Blackbodies, glow-worms,
ghosts of radiation:

I track and root out heat,
its absorption and emission,
the white bed's infra-red, the bright
spoor of the soul's transmission.

THE LONG HOME

I hadn't been back in twenty years
and he was still here, by the fire,
at the far end of the longest bar-counter
in Aberdeen – some say Scotland.
Not many in, and my favourite time:
the dog-watch; the city still working,
its tortoiseshell light just legible
in the smoked windows,
and through the slow delay of glass
the streetlights
batting into life.

The firewood's sap
buzzing like a trapped fly,
the granular crackle of a *Green Final*
folded and unfolded,
the sound of the coals
unwrapping themselves like sweets.
He only looked up when the barman
poured a bucketful of ice
into the sink, like a tremendous
burst of applause.

He was drinking Sweetheart Stout
and whisky, staring into the glass
of malt as if it were the past, occasionally
taking a pull on the long brown bottle.
I remember him telling me,
with that grim smile,

'I'm washing my wounds in alcohol.'
I liked a drink too,
but would always leave before him,
walking home, as if on a wire.

I'd heard what had happened
but wasn't ready for the terrible wig,
all down at one side, the turn
in his mouth and his face's
hectic blaze. He'd left here so bad
he could barely stand.
He'd got through his door, back to his room
and passed out for the night,
sleeping like a log with his head in the fire.

SORROWS

An over-filled glass:
I take my head
in my hands,
careful not to spill.

*

Without a real death in my life
I had to make my own.

Now I build models of my father
out of smoke and light.

*

He was uncomfortable,
so I asked the nurse
if we could lift him higher.
He died an hour later.
Usually happens, she explained,
after you move them.
Forgive me, I say, at his feet,
through a mouthful of nails.

*

In his shirt-sleeves and flannels
I remember him:

a stitch in his side
from the long run home.

*

The dam he built
in the stream is finally broken:
cold Highland water
rushing to the sea.

WAVES

I have swum too far
out of my depth
and the sun has gone;

the hung weight of my legs
a plumb-line,
my fingers raw, my arms lead;

the currents pull like weed
and I am very tired
and cold, and moving out to sea.

The beach is still bright.
The children I never had
run to the edge

and back to their beautiful mother
who smiles at them, looks up
from her magazine, and waves.

HIDE

I have been waiting for the black deer
all my life, hidden here in the dark
corner of the wood.
I see glimpses of them, breaking cover,
swinging away
to erase themselves in the deep trees.

They are implicit there, and will move
only if I hold still.
Though in a dream I have
they stand so near I can feel them breathing.
Then, when I look down,
I have disappeared.

Out at the wood's edge, the snorts
and coughs of the feeding herd.
A gust startles a lift of leaves, and they
scatter and bound like the far-off heads
of deer in the distance.
The wind drops and the trees are antlered.

ASTERION AND THE GOD

nec enim praesentior illo est deus

Asterion, his name is, King of Stars.
Some joke of his father's, who now
stables him here in these spiralled halls,
this walled-up palace, where shame
cries itself to sleep.

Where is my mother? Why
has she left me here alone?
This is a house of many corners
but only one room, made of stone.
I live inside this stone.

See how he prowls and paces,
my beast of a boy; moving round
his world, looking at his emptiness
from new directions.
He will have a visitor soon.

Poor monster, pulling at himself,
the DNA unspooling from his hand:
white butterflies
spill into the dark.
Out of the broken comes forth brine.

Sometimes children visit, to dance here
and play leapfrog, singing loudly,
full of wine; but they break so easily
and then it is very quiet again.
Where did I lose my life?

Fretting all night at a red bone,
he makes a mirror from the slick
and sees himself, at last, in the stone
of the running walls: lustral,
horned, bearded with blood.

I hear through the walls what I am,
what I do; sparagmos, *they call it,*
whatever that is.
They say a stranger comes
to release me. Let him come soon.

She pledged herself to me, but now
carries the crown I gave her
to light the stranger's way. The hero
who has come to kill Asterion:
her half-brother, my son. My self.

They betray each other so perfectly:
husband to wife, wife to husband;
sister to half-brother, and now
lover to lover. The symmetries
of chaos and bliss. The mysteries.

I am the true vine,
I am the fennel stalk;
and he will be honey:
buried to the horns, his body
home to the bee-swarm.

She has gone, now, with her hero,
who is already forgetting her.
I, however, never forget. She will hang
in the night sky like a princess
from a clew of twine.

Sometimes we speak, sometimes
we let the gods speak through us.
I am half; he is twice-born.
My grief still here
and I am gone.

Imagine me as the wind – the force
animals and birds know
is there, but does not threaten:
part of their world, but other.
The god who comes; the god who disappears.

FALL

after Rilke

The leaves are falling, falling from trees
in dying gardens far above us; as if their slow
free-fall was the sky declining.

And tonight, this heavy earth is falling away
from all the other stars, drawing into silence.

We are all falling now. My hand, my heart,
stall and drift in darkness, see-sawing down.

And we still believe there is one who sifts and holds
the leaves, the lives, of all those softly falling.

THE PARK DRUNK

He opens his eyes to a hard frost,
the morning's soft amnesia of snow.

The thorned stems of gorse
are starred crystal; each bud
like a candied fruit, its yellow
picked out and lit
by the low pulse
of blood-orange
riding in the eastern trees.

What the snow has furred
to silence, uniformity,
frost amplifies, makes singular:
giving every form a sound,
an edge, as if
frost wants to know what
snow tries to forget.

And so he drinks for winter,
for the coming year,
to open all the beautiful tiny doors
in their craquelure of frost;
and he drinks
like the snow falling, trying
to close the biggest door of all.

AT DAWN

I took a new path off the mountain
to this ruined croft, and went inside
to find, under the trestle table,
the earth floor seething with ants;
on the mantelpiece,
some wire-wool, a box of screws,
a biscuit-tin of human hair
and a urine sample
with my name and date of birth.
In each corner, something else:
five blackthorn pins beside
five elder twigs, freshly cut
and red at both ends, tied up
with ribbons into the shape of a man;
the blade-bone of a sheep; a mackerel
wrapped in today's paper, one eye
looking up at me
through its greased window;
the lopped head of a roe deer,
its throat full of wire.
The last thing I found
was a photograph of me,
looking slightly younger,
stretched out, on a trestle table.

WHAT THE HORSES SEE AT NIGHT

When the day-birds have settled
in their creaking trees,
the doors of the forest open
for the flitting
drift of deer
among the bright croziers
of new ferns
and the legible stars;
foxes stream from the earth;
a tawny owl
sweeps the long meadow.
In a slink of river-light,
the mink's face
is already slippery with yolk,
and the bay's
tiny islands are drops
of solder
under a drogue moon.
The sea's a heavy sleeper,
dreaming in and out with a catch
in each breath, and is not disturbed
by that *plowt* – the first
in a play of herring, a shoal
silvering open
the sheeted black skin of the sea.
Through the starting rain, the moon
skirrs across the sky dragging
torn shreds of cloud behind.

The fox's call is red
and ribboned
in the snow's white shadow.
The horses watch the sea climb
and climb and walk
towards them on the hill,
hear the vole
crying under the alder,
our children
breathing slowly in their beds.

TRYSTS

meet me
where the sun goes down
meet me
in the cave, under the battleground
meet me
on the broken branch
meet me
in the shade, below the avalanche
meet me
under the witch's spell
meet me
tonight, in the wishing well
meet me
on the famine lawn
meet me
in the eye of the firestorm
meet me
in your best shoes
and your favourite dress
meet me
on your own, in the wilderness
meet me
as my lover, as my only friend
meet me
on the river bed

PRIMAVERA

for Cait

The Brimstone is back
in the woken hills of Vallombrosa,
passing the word
from speedwell to violet
wood anemone to celandine.
I could walk to you now
with Spring just ahead of me,
north over flat ground
at two miles an hour,
the sap moving with me,
under the rising
grass of the field
like a dragged magnet,
the lights of the flowers
coming on in waves
as I walked with the budburst
and the flushing of trees.
If I started now,
I could bring you the Spring
for your birthday.

THE DEATH OF ACTAEON

after Ovid

for James Lasdun

Noon: midsummer; Mount Cithaeron.
The baking ground is brown with the blood of beasts, drained
since dawn by Actaeon and his men; their nets
are stiff with it. It cakes their hands and spear-shafts.
Enough for one day, they head for shade to dream of water.

*

There was a deep cleft in the mountain, meshed
with cypresses and pine; in it, a distant
speck of glass: the sacred pool.
Hot from the hunt, the huntress-queen
would come to this grove
to cool herself in the pure water:
daughter of Zeus, twin sister of Apollo, protectress
of these wild woods and these mountains:
the virgin goddess, Artemis.

Twenty Amnisian nymphs attend their queen.
As she steps into the pool, they stand aside
while the deftest folds the locks of hair into a knot.
Scooping a palmful of water to her neck and throat,
letting it run the length of her, she straightens in the sunlight,
her back's curve bending like a longbow
as she raises her arms to unbind the knot,

shake loose her hair
and stretch.

Arms outspread,
one step at a time,
he inched down
through the cooling air,
to enter
– though he did not know it –
the grove of Artemis.
He parted the branches,
slipping through ferns
that dripped with spray,
and reached the grassy bank
and the murmur of voices, or water.
Edging into the open,
he saw stillness,
and grace, in the space of one heartbeat;
then he saw his own death.

Like gazelles at a waterhole sensing a lion,
the handmaidens turned their heads
and the glass split.
Light went everywhere
– into the screams as they covered their breasts,
into the water, as they thrashed it white,
crowding round their goddess, trying
to hide her body with their own.
But she stood too high above them, and began to burn –
and turned away, glaring over her shoulder,
as if to reach for an arrow
from a quiver that wasn't there.

There was no weapon but water.
Enraged, she caught up a handful
and flung it in his face,
leaving a trail of gold as she spoke these words:
'Now go and tell, if you can,
that you have seen the goddess Artemis naked.'

With that, a rack of branching stag horns
burst from his wet brow.
Actaeon felt his bones stretch and the sinews snap
as she lengthened his neck, drew the tips of his ears to a point,
put hooves in place of hands and feet,
turned his arms into forelegs that reached and lunged
as his hind legs tensed and gathered,
and thickened his pale skin to a brindled hide.
And last of all she poured a white fear into his heart
like a stream of other blood. And it was done.

He fled.
Sharp hooves bit into the ground,
horns clattering the branches –
plunging out across the grove in springs and bounds
he was amazed by his own lightness.
But when he saw his antlered head
looking back at him from a mountain pool, he knew
only his mind remained – and it was scattered –
torn between running home to the palace,
or hiding out here in the woods; torn between shame and fear.

As he hesitated, the dogs caught his trail
and decided for him: first to give tongue were Blackclaw
and keen-scented Tracer, never mistaken:
Tracer a Cretan dog, Blackclaw a Spartan; then others
came rushing on, wave on successive wave:
Stag-chaser, Ravener, Fell-ranger – all from Arcadia –
Fawnbane the fawn-killer, Hurricane and Death-bringer,
Wingfeet, the swift of foot, Hunter the hungry,
the boar-scarred Sylvan, Harrier the wolf-dog,
Shepherd the rallier; Grappler with her black kin,
Catcher from Sicyon, thin in the flank; Runner and Courser,
Blazon and Tiger, the roistering Ravager,
white-coated Frost-biter and black-haired Mourner,
and fast at their shoulders, famed for his strength, came Spartan,
and Tempest, renowned for his stamina,
Wildfire and Wolf-taker with her brother The Cyprian,
Grasper with his white star, Bristler and Blackbeard,
Lightfoot and White-tooth, shrill-tongued Ring-the-Wood,
And others, many others, it would take too long to name.

Locked on to their quarry,
the whole pack, thick with bloodlust,
flowed over the rocks and crags, over the trackless cliffs
– where the way is hard, or where there is no way at all.
He leapt and jinked through the killing grounds
longing to cry out: 'I am Actaeon!
Don't you know your own master?' but there was no sound
but the baying of dogs; the air cracked with their barking.
And then they came.
The three out-runners spilled through the trees to outstrip the others.

Hellhound clamped his teeth – with two puffs of red –
into his master's back, then Deerkiller and Hill-Fury
latched to his shoulder and hung on.

While they held down their prey,
the rest of the pack broke on him like surf,
dipping their teeth into his flesh
till there was no place left for further wounds,
and at every wound's mouth was the mouth of a dog.
Surge upon surge, the riptide crashed and turned,
battening on, and tearing away – maddened – in the red spume.
Actaeon groaned: a sound which wasn't human,
but which no stag could produce.
Falling to his knees, like a supplicant at prayer, he bowed
in silence as the angry sea crashed on him once again
and the dogs hid his body with their own.
Drowning now,
his horned head reared, streaming, from the ruck,
as if a god was being born
– not a mortal soul transformed and torn apart.
The huntsmen looked around for Actaeon: calling
– each louder than the one before – for Actaeon,
as if he weren't there.
Should he not share this unexpected gift?
This sixteen-pointer brought to bay?
Actaeon turned his head at the sound of his name.
He wished he were as far away as they thought;
or watching this death, not living it.
And his dogs kept swivelling round to look for their master,
barking their signal for him to come,

come and dispatch the beast they'd brought down;
and Actaeon turned again.
Then for the last time
the thirsty hounds surrounded him,
closed over him,
worked their heads into his body,
and tore him, inside out.
Then, and only then, they say,
was the anger of Artemis, goddess of chastity, appeased.

*

It is also said that the dogs devoured the body, then hunted
for Actaeon in vain throughout the forest. Finally their search
brought them to the cave of Chiron the centaur, who had
fostered Actaeon as a child and taught him how to hunt. Only
after he had fashioned a statue of their lost master could the
dogs be calmed and allow themselves to be led home.

SWIMMING IN THE WOODS

Her long body in the spangled shade of the wood
was a swimmer moving through a pool:
fractal, finned by leaf and light;
the loose plates of lozenge and rhombus
wobbling coins of sunlight.
When she stopped, the water stopped,
and the sun re-made her as a tree,
banded and freckled and foxed.

Besieged by symmetries, condemned
to these patterns of love and loss,
I stare at the wet shape on the tiles
till it fades; when she came and sat next to me
after her swim and walked away
back to the trees, she left a dark butterfly.

GHOST OF A GARDEN

Sometimes I discover I have gone downstairs,
crossed the grass and found myself
in here: the tool-shed,
caught in a lash of brambles, bindweed
and tall ivied trees like pipecleaners. It looks out,
vacantly, on a garden run to seed:
the lost tennis court, grown-over benches,
a sunken barbecue snagged with blown roses.
The courtyard walls are full of holes the swallows
try to sew, in and out of them like open doors.
In the corner of the shed my father is weeping
and I cannot help him because he is dead.

SELKIE

in memory of Michael Donaghy

'I'm not stopping,'
he said, shrugging off his skin
like a wet-suit, then stretching it
on the bodhrán's frame,
'let's play.'
And he played till dawn:
all the jigs and reels
he knew, before he stood
and drained the last
from his glass, slipped back in
to the seal-skin,
into a new day, saluting us
with that famous grin:
'That's me away.'

WORMWOOD

for Don Paterson

A flight of loose stairs off the street into a high succession
of empty rooms, prolapsed chairs and a memory of women
perfumed with hand-oil and *Artemisia absinthium*:
wormwood to me, and to the sappy Russian sailors, *chernobyl*.
The scooped-back ballroom gown
shows the tell-tale bra-strap, red and tired.
'Leave it,' my maths master used to say at a dropped pencil,
'it can't fall any further.' Well, I couldn't, and neither could she.

THE GLAIR

The slow drag across the sandpaper,
scratching smoke
from the head of the match
again and again until it flares.
Lamplight lies heavy on her breasts,
her flanks; the hand's passage
slow as ceremony, persistent
as a dream unsleeved; the spark
drawn in hard with a catch
of flame: the lumbering storm
and the white bolt, the bright rope, on
and on and on. The albumen. The glair.

HEEL OF BREAD

The spatter of rain
at the window

sounds
like crackling flames;

the writhe and twist
as you

slit yourself on me,
riding my hand.

Rain
flails against the glass.

I have made
a litter of my life.

No news, no
new descent:

It's over, you said,
this is the last time.

I consider
the wine-stains,

the obligatory
heel of bread.

NEW YORK SPRING

Couples strolling
through stopped light,
the cherry's slew of blossom, those
fallen shells of pink magnolia,
the inconsolable sadness of this
Saturday in Central Park.

The trail gone
under the blossom and I think
of all my loves and how I lost them,
walking the only path
allowed to me
from all the roads I chose.

Beyond the lake
an accordion's slow polka, its broken
soundtrack foundering,
stopping, starting over;
the girls have all gone home now,
I know, I don't need to be told.
The dance finished
twenty years ago.

MYTH

This morning, in bracken
beyond the east field,
I find the blown bulbs of sunset;
on the wet lawn,
after the snow,
the snowman's spine.

THE LAKE AT DUSK

I watch the day break down
over the lake: wind
looting the trees,
leaving paw-prints on the water
for the water-witch to read.

With the pass of a hand
it stops,
and the scoured lake
lies pewter-still
in a red, raking light, now
hardening to mirror.

Rinsed after the rain,
the forest is triggered and tripwired;
when I pause for a bird call
the silence takes time
to reassemble around me
like a dream retrieved.
No one will find me here.

The ditches churn with frogs
and the track is lit
with their green and yellow
flattened stars.
Some let a cloudy scribble
milk out from their sides, like semen;

all of them carry the same rubric,
legible and bright.

The reed-pool trembles,
as if for a god.
Night switches through the trees.

In the open dark
all maps are useless:
the tracks are bloodied;
the tracks are washed clean.
Is this a way through the forest,
this path? Is this the way I came?

A SEAGULL MURMUR

is what they called it,
shaking their heads
like trawlermen;

the mewling sound of a leaking heart
            the sound
of a gull trapped in his chest.

To let it out
they ran a cut down his belly
like a fish, his open ribs

the ribs of a boat;
            and they closed him,
wired him shut.

Caulked and sea-worthy now
with his new valve; its metal
tapping away:

the dull clink
            of a signal-buoy
or a beak at the bars of a cage.

ACTAEON: THE EARLY YEARS

A museum etiquette of table-mat and coaster,
ornaments that stayed put for decades: milkmaids,
donkeys, a weeping shepherdess and her china sheep;
it was a craft-shop Arcadia in a headache of pastels:
a shrine to hygiene and disappointment, a grief
he tiptoed through for years.

*

Her migraines were his fault, being the wrong child.
The best way, folk said, to be rid of changelings,
was to burn them with peat – send them hissing
up the chimney. The true child would be there by the fire
the next day. Not keeping turf, for the mess
it made, she used boiling milk, but it failed.

*

In his blue smock, sitting in a shambles
of coloured paper: 'You've ruined everything!'
she screamed, ruining everything.
The glue-bottle had a raw mouth
slit in its red rubber; he stabbed the table with it,
wanting to glue the world to bits.

*

A shore-dweller, he haunted the harled beach
with its broken toys, sucking boiled sweets
like sea glass. Once, after paddling,
he wanted to walk home nude

and fell – or was pushed – into a nettle-ditch.
She sewed him a suit of dock-leaves.

*

His first death was on holiday, in a boy-sized
hole in the ground topped with corrugated iron
and brambles. He was dead all afternoon,
moist in the teeming dark, and had never been
so happy, alone there, untraceable. He hated
the hunger that brought him back to life.

*

He stood waiting beside her as she talked
on the new telephone – a four-year-old
admiring her growing bulge. 'Look, Mummy,'
he said, 'now you have two bumps,'
meaning her breasts and her pregnancy.
She turned and knocked him to the floor.

*

He learnt that desire for intimacy
was a transgression, and that
the resulting fear of intimacy,
which was also now a fear of disclosure,
was understandable, even natural,
in this place, among these people.

*

The dunes were wired in a mesh of marram grass
and steel. The wind whittled the children thin and white

as they pleitered in the shallows with the dead crabs,
while the grown-ups shivered into their thermos flasks
behind wind-breaks and tank-traps,
shouting down to them to mind the dog-mess and the glass.

*

A man was standing over her, still dripping from the sea;
she looked up from the hand she was cradling in her lap,
to the boy in the doorway: her left thumb
pincushioned with the steel heads of dress-making pins
silvering the red meat. 'Pull them out,' said the swimmer
in the dream, 'every one, and your mother will be better.'

*

There was the comfort of sherbet fountains
and aniseed balls, foam bananas in wax-paper cones;
running home with a block of vanilla
wrapped in newspaper; the Sunday treat of a poke of chips
after seeing the grandparents. Best of all
the saved-up, sudden, consolation of chocolate.

*

He passed a slaughterhouse on the way to school:
a hall of cold columns, cream and red,
all turning slowly on their hooks.
He blessed himself: stunned at the passion, this
breaking-open, the rough grain of the blood sliding
between forefinger and thumb.

*

Some teachers customised the leather tawse they used
to beat the children's hands, frilling the end with a craft-knife.
'This is going to hurt me more than it will hurt you.'
On the pocket of his blazer, the school crest
was a pelican in her piety, feeding her young
with blood from her own breast.

*

You could smell the herring-catch come in each morning,
taste sea-salt on everything. Some folk swam
before they walked, they say, like his first girlfriend
with her lucken toes – said
to bring good fortune, show
that seal-blood sang in the veins.

*

From the top of the monkey puzzle, lit by the arced bow
of a new moon, he saw her, lying there in the bath: the white
face-mask first, then the rest. That hair. She must have
screamed as she covered her breasts because her face
chipped open, like her favourite porcelain fawn, the one
the cleaner broke. The hole at the muzzle like a smile, almost.

*

Hiding in the trees for hours was how he used to disappear:
that absence in the high-leafed branches, the canopy
opened to a sea of sky. Later, it was a well-shaft:
the tree inverted, sunk; he climbed down into its dark
and sat in the mulch of foliage, the black stars capsized,
his life capsized; his need to vanish, drowned.

*

When he left, he left no stain of himself on the paintwork's
magnolia, the carpets' analgesic-blue.
No sign or spoor. Twenty years spent
edging past a migraine's darkened room. He slipped a note
into a gap in the floorboards:
'all the roads I walk will be away from you.'

LEAVINGS

Still sleepwalking through your life,
I wrap you up
and we go through the snow that fell all night
and all through this Christmas morning:
your trainers barely denting the whitened lawn, your
two strides for every stride of mine.

Leaving you home
to the warmth of the house
I step back out, and see where my footprints turn
and walk through yours,
the other way – following the trail
of rabbit and deer into the unreachable silences of snow.
I can bring nothing of this back intact.
My face is smoke, my body water,
my tracks are made of snow.

The next morning is a dripping thaw, and winter
is gone from the grass – except for a line
of white marks going nowhere:
the stamped ellipses of impacted snow;
everything gone, leaving just this, this ghost-tread,
these wafer-thin footsteps of glass.

DONEGAL

for Eilidh

Ardent on the beach at Rossnowlagh
on the last day of summer,
you ran through the shallows
throwing off shoes, and shirt and towel
like the seasons, the city's years,
all caught in my arms
as I ploughed on behind you, guardian still
of dry clothes, of this little heart
not quite thirteen,
breasting the waves
and calling back to me
to join you, swimming in the Atlantic
on the last day of summer.
I saw a man in the shallows
with his hands full of clothes, full of
all the years,
and his daughter going
where he knew he could not follow.

LA STANZA DELLE MOSCHE

The room sizzles in the morning sun;
a tinnitus of flies at the bright windows,
butting and dunting the glass. One dings
off the light, to the floor, vibrating blackly,
pittering against the wall before taxi
and take-off – another low moaning flight,
another fruitless stab at the world outside.
They drop on my desk, my hands,
and spin their long deaths on their backs
on the white tiles, first one way
then the other, tiny humming tops that
stop and start: a sputter of bad wiring,
whining to be stubbed out.

LIZARD

Volatile hybrid of dinosaur and toy, this
living remnant throbs on the hot stone:
a prehistoric offcut, six inches
of chlorophyll-green dusted with pollen;
a trick of nature – lithe, ectopic, cuneiform –
a stocking-filler, out of place everywhere
but in the sun. Frisking the wall,
its snatched run is a dotted line
of fits and starts, spasmodic, end-stopped.
It pulses once; slips into a rock with a gulp.

CROSSING THE ARCHIPELAGO

Rising in November in these days of dusk
I am one life older, watching now as the walls
green over, the stones break into bud;
if this is ebb-tide turned to flood it means that
nightfall might begin again at dawn.
And so it does. The sea at Djurgården is a mirror
of lost light. I watch snowflakes fall on water,
transparent as tissue, melting back to nothing,
the black water's endless echo of the night.
A diminished life turns turtle and the day breaks
like a spell; to double back on this, through
ash and silver birch, to that extinguished past, a world
that's over, will wreck me. Hopeless to return
now: my future lit by bridges, and their burning.

RAINMAKER

Tentative rain, and the light
is changing, the water ticking
in the leaves, pattering the sheets
as she turns to him, murmuring
slow and ready for the verge of flood,
the undertow's hard covenant,
the run of trust.
She feels something unfurling
in a glut of dew, a finger pushing
into a peach, peach-water welling
over fern and fruit; she tastes the curve
and ache in the weather.
He unhooks her, and
leaning in
he starts to make her rain.

HOLDING PROTEUS

Becalmed here
on this salt beach far from home,
my boat blisters and flakes in the sun;
it has forgotten the sea
as I have forgotten the sea's purpose,
which is to change.
Sea-voyager, law-maker, warrior,
I walk in my own footprints now
around this island,
around myself, waiting for wind, trying
to hazard the heart's meridian,
a draught of air, a star to steer by.

My hands have been still for so long
they can't tell what they hold.

I've tried to buy the wind with coins
thrown from the water's edge, whistled
till my lips were raw, taken a whip
to the ship's boy, cut a pig's throat
with my own sword, sung
each of the supplicant songs,
untied all three magic knots in the cord
– no breeze, no wind, no storm.
The sea is deadpan.
I have worshipped the wrong gods.

I fall asleep over my book
of maps and legends, and I am char,
I am the fire-flags in the ashes of the field,
black-drowned in the marl-pit,
the unstrung heretic crouched in marram.
I am that rocking grief, those numb limbs.
I am the child, abandoned on the beach.

You turn, in my arms, to a deer,
a dolphin, shivering aspen, tiger, eel,
lithe root of flame and broken water.
I hold you fast, until you are flesh again,
seal-herder, seer, sea-guardian:
you who can only tell the truth,
show me how to find a fresh wind
and a safe harbour.

I wake to sea-storm, sunstorm, bright waves;
the sea-wind tearing pages from my book.

TRUMPETER SWAN

He takes a run at it: heaving himself
up off the lake, wing-beats echoing,
the wheeze of each pull
pulling him clear.

The sky is empty;
every stretch of water
flaunts its light.

You can learn how to fly, see all the edges
soften and blur, but you can't hold on
to the height you find,
you can never be taught how to fall.

ALBUM

I am almost never there, in these
old photographs: a hand
or shoulder, out of focus; a figure
in the background,
stepping from the frame.
I see myself, sometimes, in the restless
blur of a child, that flinch
in the eye, or the way
sun leaks its gold into the print;
or there, in that long white gash
across the face of the glass
on the wall behind. That
smear of light
the sign of me, leaving.

Look closely
at these snapshots, all this
Kodacolor going to blue, and you'll
start to notice. When you finally see me,
you'll see me everywhere: floating
over crocuses, sandcastles,
fallen leaves, on those
melting snowmen, their faces
drawn in coal – among all
the wedding guests,
the dinner guests, the birthday-
party guests – this smoke
in the emulsion, the flaw.
A ghost is there; the ghost gets up to go.

SIGNS ON A WHITE FIELD

The sun's hinge on the burnt horizon
has woken the sealed lake,
leaving a sleeve of sound. No wind,
just curved plates of air
re-shaping under the trap-ice,
straining to give; the groans and rumbles
like someone shifting heavy tables far below.
I snick a stone over the long sprung deck
to get the dobro's glassy note, the crying
slide of a bottleneck, its
tremulous ululation to the other shore.
The rocks are ice-veined; the trees
swagged with snow.
Here and there, a sudden frost
has caught some turbulence in the water
and made it solid: frozen in its distress
to a scar, or a skin-graft.
Everywhere, frost-heave has jacked up boulders
clear of the surface, and the ice-shove
has piled great slabs on the lake-edge
like luggage tumbled from a carousel.

A racket of jackdaws, the serrated call
of a falcon as I walk out onto the lake.

A living lens of ice; you can hear it bending,
breathing, re-adjusting its weight and light
as the hidden tons of water
swell and stretch underneath,
thickening with cold.

A low grumble, a lingering vibrato, creaks
that seem to echo back and forth for hours;
the lake is talking to itself. A loud
twang in the ice. Twitterings
in the railway lines
from a train about to arrive.
A pencilled-in silence,
hollow and provisional.
And then it comes.
The detonating crack, like a dropped plank,
as if the whole lake has snapped in two
and the world will follow.
But all that happens
is a huge release of sound: a boom
that rolls under the ice for miles,
some fluked leviathan let loose
from centuries of sleep, trying to push through,
shaking the air like sheet metal,
like a muffled giant drum.

I hear the lake all night like a distant war.
In the morning's brightness
I brush the snow off with a glove,
smooth down a porthole in the crust
and find, somehow, the living green beneath.
The green leaf looks back, and sees
a man walking out in this shuddering light
to the sound of air under the ice,
out onto the lake, among sun-cups,
snow penitents: a drowned man, waked
in this weathering ground.

BY CLACHAN BRIDGE

for Alasdair Roberts

I remember the girl
with the hare-lip
down by Clachan Bridge,
cutting up fish
to see how they worked;
by morning's end her nails
were black red, her hands
all sequined silver.
She unpuzzled rabbits
to a rickle of bones;
dipped into a dormouse
for the pip of its heart.
She'd open everything,
that girl.
They say they found
wax dolls in her wall,
poppets full of human hair,
but I'd say they're wrong.
What's true is
that the blacksmith's son,
the simpleton,
came down here once
and fathomed her.
Claimed she licked him
clean as a whistle.
I remember the tiny stars
of her hands around her belly

as it grew and grew, and how
after a year, nothing came.
How she said it was still there,
inside her, a stone-baby.
And how I saw her wrists
bangled with scars
and those hands flittering
at her throat,
to the plectrum of bone
she'd hung there.
As to what happened
to the blacksmith's boy,
no one knows
and I'll keep my tongue.
Last thing I heard, the starlings
had started
to mimic her crying,
and she'd found how to fly.

THE PLAGUE YEAR

Great elms gesture in the last of the light. I am dying
so slowly you'd hardly notice. What is there left
to trust but this green world and its god,
always returning to life? I stood
all day in the vanishing point; my place
now taken by a white-tailed deer.

*

I go to check the children, who are done for.
They lie there broken on their beds, limbs thrown out
in the attitudes of death, the shape of soldiers.
The next morning, I look up at my reflection
in the train window: unshaven, with today's paper;
behind me stands a gunman in a hood.

*

The chestnut trees hold out their breaking buds
like lanterns, or wounds, sticky with life. Under the
false-teeth-whistling flight of a wood-pigeon
a thrown wave of starlings rose and sank itself
back into a hedge, in a burst of chatter.
My father in the heart of the hedge, clasping a bible.

*

Rain muscles its way through the gutters
of Selma and Vine. I look north
through the fog at the Hollywood sign,
east to the observatory where tonight,
under a lack of stars,
old men will be fighting with knives.

*

Western Michigan,
on the Pere Marquette
roll-casting for steelhead:
mending my line over a drift of them
stitched into the shadows,
looking for a loophole in the water.

*

Descending a wrought-iron spiral stair, peering
down at the people very far below;
no hand-rail, every
second step rusted away, I'm holding
a suitcase and a full glass of wine,
wearing carpet slippers and a Balenciaga gown.

*

My past stretches from here to there, and back,
leaving me somewhere in the middle
of Shepherd's Bush Green with the winos of '78.
A great year; I remember it well. Hints of petrol,
urine, plane trees; a finish so long you could
sleep out under it. Same faces, different names.

*

Parrots tear out their feathers, whistling Jingle Bells,
cornfields burst into flames, rivers dry
from their source to the sea, snakes sun themselves
as the roads return to tar; puffer fish off the Lizard,
whales in the Thames, the nets heavy
with swordfish, yellowfin, basking shark.

*

Cyclamen under olive trees, sacked tombs, a ruined
moussaka, with chips. Locals on motorbikes
chew pitta bread, stare out at me like sheep,
their wayside shrines to the saints
built better than their houses; at every bend
tin memorials to the crashed dead.

*

I was down here in the playground
with the other adults,
on the roundabouts and swings,
while up on the hill
on the tennis court,
the children were kneeling to be shot.

*

In November, two ring-necked parakeets
eating from apples still hanging
from the apple tree. The dead crow I notice
is just a torn black bin-liner;
at the end of the garden a sand-pit stands up
as a fox, and slopes off.

*

Smoked mackerel, smoked eel, smoked halibut,
smoked reindeer heart, veal pâté, six different kinds
of salmon, Gustav's Sausage, Jansson's Temptation.
Tasting each *ex voto*, I saw the electrodes
in a bucket, the blade, the gaff, the captive bolt,
walking my plate around the stations of the dead.

TULIPS

Sifting sand in the Starsign Hotel
on 96th and Madison,
trying not to hear the sirens: the heart's
fist, desire's empty hand.
The room awash with its terrible light;
a sky unable to rain. Cradling a glass
of nothing much at all, it's all
come down to this: the electric fan's
stop-start – the stalled, half-circle twist
of draught over the bed; the sea-spill
of sheets, the head in storm. Look
at what's beached here on the night-stand:
a flipped photograph and a silk scarf, a set
of keys. These tulips, loosening in a vase.

WONDERLAND

She said her name was Alice,
that she'd studied with the geisha
in Japan, and was trained and able
in the thousand ways of pleasuring a man.
We'd share some shots of whisky
– her favourite brand, *Black Label* –
then she'd knock them back, and drink me
under the table.

THE TWEED

Giving a back-rub
to Hugh MacDiarmid
I felt, through the tweed,
so much tension
in that determined
neck, those little
bony shoulders
that, when it was released,
he simply
stood up and fell over.

ABOUT TIME

In the time it took to hold my breath
and slip under the bathwater
– to hear the blood-thud in the veins,
for me to rise to the surface –
my parents had died,
the house had been sold and now
was being demolished around me,
wall by wall, with a ball and chain.

I swim one length underwater,
pulling myself up on the other side, gasping,
to find my marriage over,
my daughters grown and settled down,
the skin loosening
from my legs and arms
and this heart going
like there's no tomorrow.

CAT, FAILING

A figment, a thumbed
maquette of a cat, some
ditched plaything, something
brought in from outside:
his white fur stiff and grey,
coming apart at the seams.
I study the muzzle
of perished rubber, one ear
eaten away, his sour body
lumped like a bean-bag
leaking thinly
into a grim towel. I sit
and watch the light
degrade in his eyes.

He tries and fails
to climb to his chair, shirks
in one corner of the kitchen,
cowed, denatured, ceasing to be
anything like a cat,
and there's a new look
in those eyes
that refuse to meet mine
and it's the shame of being
found out. Just that.
And with that
loss of face
his face, I see,
has turned human.

A GIFT

She came to me in a dress
of true-love and blue rocket,
with fairy-thimbles of foxglove
at the neck and wrist,
in her hair she wore a garland
of cherry laurel, herb bennet,
dwayberries and yew-berries,
twined with stems of clematis,
and at her throat she'd threaded
twists of bryony stalk, seeds
of meadow saffron and laburnum,
linked simply in a necklace,
and she was holding out
a philtre of water lovage,
red chamomile and ladies' seal
in a cup, for me to drink.

STRINDBERG IN BERLIN

All the wrong turnings
that have brought me here –
debts, divorce, a court trial, and now
a forced exile in this city and this drinking cell,
Zum Schwarzen Ferkel, The Black Piglet:
neither home nor hiding-place, just
another indignity,
just a different make of hell.

Outside, a world of people queuing
to stand in my light, and that sound
far in the distance, of my life
labouring to catch up.
I've now pulled out
every good tooth
in search of the one that was making me mad.
I squint at the flasks and alembics,
head like a wasps' nest,
and pour myself
three fingers and a fresh start.
A glass of *aqua vitae*, a straightener,
stiffener, a universal tincture – same again –
the great purifier, clarifier,
a steadying hand on the dancing hand,
– one more, if you wouldn't mind –
bringer of spirit and the spirit of love;
the cleansing fire, turning lead
to gold, the dead back into life.

The Pole at the piano, of course;
Munch opposite me, his face
like a shirt done up wrong.
My fiancée in one corner, my lover in another,
merging, turning, as all women turn,
back into my daughters,
and I am swimming naked at night,
off the island, in the witch-fire of *mareld* light,
listening to the silence of the stars,
with my children beside me,
my beautiful lost children, in the swell
of the night, swimming beside me.

And back, to the bright salts and acids,
the spill and clamour of the bar,
the elixirs, the women:
my wife-to-be, my young lover –
one banked hearth, one unattended fire.
Christ. The hot accelerant of drink.
The rot of desire.
And out, out into the swinging dark,
a moon of mercury, lines of vitriol trees
and the loose earth that rises up,
drops on me, burying me,
night after night after night.

VENERY

What is he to think now,
the white scut
of her bottom
disappearing
down the half-flight
carpet stair
to the bathroom?
What is he to do
with this masted image?
He put all his doubt
to the mouth of her long body,
let her draw the night
out of him like a thorn.
She touched it, and it moved: that's all.

MY GIRLS

How many times
have I lain alongside them
willing them to sleep
after the same old stories;
face to face, hand in hand,
till they smooth into dream and I can
slip these fingers free
and drift downstairs:
my face a blank,
hands full of deceit.

LEAVING ST KILDA

Clouds stream over the edge of Mullach Mòr, pouring
into the valley as we sail against the sun from Village Bay,
rounding the Point, and the Point of the Water,
north under Oiseval and the Hill of the Wind, and round
past the Skerry of the Cormorants, the Cleft
of the Sea-Shepherd, and out around the Yellow Headland
to The Hoof, and the Cleft of the Hoof, to The Gap
where the fulmars nest in their sorrel and chickweed;
and on to Stac a'Langa, the Long Stack
also called the Stack of the Guillemot, and Sgeir Dhomnuill,
place of shags, who are drying their wings like a line
of blackened tree-stumps, to Mina Stac and Bradastac
under the deep gaze of Conachair the Roarer
and Mullach Mòr the Great Summit,
and the White Summit and the Bare Summit beyond;
from there to the Cleft of the Leap, of the Ruinous Fall,
and round the promontory, and its tunnels and arches
to Geo nan Plaidean, the Cleft of the Blankets,
and Geo nan Ron, the Cleft of the Seals, to rest
by Hardship Cave and the deep doorways in the cliffs
of wide Glen Bay; the air still, the Atlantic flat as steel.
Southwards lies Gleann Mòr, the Great Glen, which holds
the Brae of Weepings, the House of the Trinity
and The Amazon's House, The Well of Many Virtues,
and also, it's said, above The Milking Stone, among
the shielings, a place they call The Plain of Spells.
Here also, the home of the great skua,
the bonxie, the harasser: pirate, fish-stealer,
brown buzzard of the sea who kills for the sake of it.

And on past the Cleft of the Lame and the Beach of the Cairn
of the Green Sword and the Chasm of the Steep Skerry
to the crest of The Cambir, and round its ridge to Soay.

Three great sea-stacks guard the gateway to the Isle of Sheep:
the first, Soay Stac, the second, Stac Dona – also called
The Stack of Doom – where nothing lives. The third – kingdom
of the fulmar, and tester of men who would climb
her sheer sides – the Pointed Stack, Stac Biorach.
Out on the ocean, they ride the curve of the wave; but here
in the air above their nests, in their thousands, they are ash
blown round a bonfire, until you see them closer, heeling
and banking. The grey keel
and slant of them: shearing,
planing the rock, as if their endless
turning of it might shape the stone –
as the sea has fashioned the overhangs
and arches, pillars, clefts and caves, through
centuries of close attention, of making its presence known.
Under the stacks, the shingle beach at Mol Shoay,
filled with puffins, petrels, shearwaters, and on the slopes
up to The Altar, the brown sheep of Soay graze.
Above the cliffs, and round again past the Red Cleft
to the rocks of Creagan, Am Plaistir, the Place of Splashing,
under the grey hill of Cnoc Glas, to the Point of the Strangers,
the Point of the Promontory, Flame Point, and beyond that
the Skerry of the Son of the King of Norway.

Back to Hirta and The Cambir to the Mouth of the Cleft
and The Cauldron Pool and down through the skerries
to the western heights of Mullach Bi – the Pillar Summit –

and Claigeann Mòr, Skull Rock.
Between them, the boulder field of Carn Mòr – sanctuary
of storm petrels, Leach's petrels, Manx shearwaters –
and up on the ridge, the Lover's Stone.
Past The Beak of the Wailer, Cleft of the Grey Cow,
the Landing Place of the Strangers, to An Torc, The Boar,
rising from the sea under Mullach Sgar and Clash na Bearnaich,
and The Notches that sit under Ruaival
the Red Fell, pink with thrift – past the white churning
at the mouth of the kyle, and on through the mists
of kittiwakes to the serrated fastness of Dùn:
The Doorpost, The Fank, the Lobster Precipice, Hamalan
the Anvil Rock, The Pig's Snout,
The Fissures, and The Beak of Dùn.

And then north-east, four miles, to the fortress of Boreray,
rising a thousand feet out of the black-finned sea.
To the northern stack: Stac an Armin, Stack of the Warrior,
highest sea-stack in these islands of Britain, where the last
great auk was killed as a witch
a hundred and seventy years ago. On its southern edge,
The Spike, Am Biran, and Broken Point – long loomery
of the guillemot – and across to The Heel,
split vertically in two, and the Cleft of Thunder.
Round, then, the heights of Boreray,
clockwise this time, round
to high Sunadal the swimmy-headed, home of puffins,
and the village of cleits
like turf-roofed chambered cairns
looking down on the Rock of the Little White Headland,
the Bay of a Woman, the Point of the Dale of the Breast,

and round the southern tip of Boreray, Gob Scapanish
– Headland of the Sheaths, Point of the Point of Caves –
and Cormorant Rock and The Cave of Ruin and then
Clagan na Rùsgachan, Skull Rock of the Fleeces,
wreathed in banner-clouds,
the Chasm of the Warrior and the great rift of Clesgor
– to reach, in the west, the Grey Stack, the Hoary Rock,
the gannetry of St Kilda: Stac Lee.
From one side a bishop's piece, from another, a shark;
all sides inches deep with guano you can smell for miles.
A stone hive of gannets, thrumming and ticking
with the machinery of sixty thousand squalling birds.
Off the rock, they open out in perfect cruciform and glide
high over the deep swell to track the shadows
of the mackerel or the herring shoal and then,
from a hundred feet, hundreds of them drop:
folding their wings
to become white javelins –
the dagger bill,
the pointed yellow head,
white body,
white wings tipped black –
they crash
white
into their own white water.

*

All eyes stay fixed
on the great sea-citadel, this
mountain range returning to the waves,

all eyes hold the gaze of the rocks
as the boat turns east – as if
to look away would break the spell –
until a shawl of mist
goes round its shoulders,
the cloud-wreaths
close over it, and it's gone.

At last we turn away, and see them
leading us: bow-riding dolphins,
our grey familiars,
and thirty gannets in a line
drawing straight from Boreray:
a gannet guard
for this far passage,
for the leaving of St Kilda.

LAW OF THE ISLAND

They lashed him to old timbers
that would barely float,
with weights at the feet so
only his face was out of the water.
Over his mouth and eyes
they tied two live mackerel
with twine, and pushed him
out from the rocks.

They stood, then,
smoking cigarettes
and watching the sky,
waiting for a gannet
to read that flex of silver
from a hundred feet up,
close its wings
and plummet-dive.

TINSEL

Tune to the frequency of the wood and you'll hear
the deer, breathing; a muscle, tensing; the sigh
of a fieldmouse under an owl. Now

listen to yourself – that friction – the push-and-drag,
the double pulse, the drum. You can hear it, clearly.
You can hear the sound of your body, breaking down.

If you're very quiet, you might pick up loss: or rather
the thin noise that losing makes – *perdition*.
If you're absolutely silent

and still, you can hear nothing
but the sound of nothing: this voice
and its wasting, the soul's tinsel. Listen . . . Listen . . .

LESSON

The green leaf opens
and the leaf falls,

each breath is a flame
that gives in to fire;

and grief is the price
we pay for love,

and the death of love
the fee of all desire.

THE WOOD OF LOST THINGS

We went walks here, as children, listening out
for gypsies, timber wolves, the great
hinges in the trees. Hours
we'd wander its long green halls
making swords from branches,
gathering stars of elderflower
to thread into a chain.
Today the forest sends up birds
to distract me, deer to turn me from the track,
puts out stems and tendrils
to trip and catch at my feet.
The sudden sun opens a path of flowers:
snowdrops, crocuses, hyacinths,
a smoke of bluebells
in the shade on either side;
a way of stamens and stigmas: the breathing
faces of flowers. I look back at the empty trees,
look up at the green, and I'm walking
through daisies and honeysuckle,
fireweed, crab apple, burnt-out
buddleia, a tangle of nettles,
berberis, bramble-wire;
the flowers gone,
just the starred calyx
and the green ovary
hardening to seed.
I take a last look at the yellow trees,
a last look at the brown, and I hear the sound
of old leaves under my feet
and the low noise of water.

I have found the place I wasn't meant to find.
The shallow creek, churning
its red and silver secrets:
failed salmon, bearded with barbs,
riding each other down;
the shore lined with baby pigeons, animals
birthing, others coming back to die.
Placenta and bones in the undergrowth,
in the clearing, in the places of drowning.
Jellyfish have taken to the woods;
mussels rope the tree-trunks.
I watch a fish flip on a thorn
in a pester of flies, one eye fixed on mine.

The wood stretched behind me, now full
of my own kind, those
who have stepped through my shadow;
a life's-worth of women in the forest corridor,
faces turned to the bark. The rows of lovers.
Mother and sister. Wife. And my daughters,
walking away into the blue distance,
turning their heads to look back.

Hung on a silver birch, my school cap
and satchel; next to them, the docken suit,
and next to that, pinned to a branch,
my lost comforter –
a piece of blanket worn to the size of my hand.
My hand as a boy. The forgotten smell of it,
the smell of myself.

And something is moving, something
held down by stones, and one by one
I see the dead unbury themselves
and take their places by the seated corpse
whose face I seem to know.
He was shivering. *It's cold*, I said.
He looked up at me and nodded, *It's cold*.
What is this place? What brings you here?
This is my home, we replied.

MIDDLE WATCH, HAMMERSMITH

He switches off the fridge
just to sit and watch
the hardness of the iced-up
ice-box start to drip,
its white block
loosening like a tooth.

BEGINNING TO GREEN

I find a kind of hope here, in this
homelessness, in this place
where no one knows me –
where I'll be gone, like some
over-wintering bird,
before they even notice.

Healed by distance
and a landscape opening
under broken sun, I like this
mirror-less, flawless world
with no people in it,
only birds.

Unmissed, I can see myself again
in this great unfurling – the song,
the fledged leaf, the wing;
in these strong trees that
twist from the bud: their grey
beginning to green.

EASTER, LIGURIA

Another day watching the ocean move
under the sun; pines, wisteria, lemon trees.
I darken this paradise like a sudden wind:
olive leaves, blown on their backs, silver
to razor-wire; cameras click in the wall.

Everyone is going home, and I realise
I have no idea what that means.
I listen to the shrieking of the gulls
and try to remember. How long ago
did I notice that the light was wrong,
that something inside me was broken?
Standing here, feeling nothing at all.
How long have I been leaving?
I don't know.

WIDOW'S WALK

On the *passeggiata*,
on the rocks
at the Marinella Bar again,
losing what remains of my language
to a thickening rain,
a week of rain
that's almost stopped the sea.
Trying to escape myself,
but there's always
someone
wanting to sew my shadow back.
The fisherman on his rock
under the red flags
has two fish in his bucket
swimming nowhere, side by side.
Lines of lacquered beetles
are rowing boats
turned upside-down;
the sea, mother-of-pearl
and broken shells;
the furled parasols
Madonnas in their shrouds.
I walk here
amongst the very old;
we watch the paint
flake from the hotel walls
and I take note, once again,
of the sign spelt out in English:

BATHING IN NOT SURE
FOR LACK OF RESCUE SERVICE.
I felt like going in,
there and then,
like a widow
toppling forward at the grave;
going in after myself.

DIVING

The sudden sea is bright
and soundless: a changed channel
of dashed colour, scrolling
plankton, sea-darts, the slope
and loom of ghosts, something
slow and grey
sashaying through a school
of cobalt blue,
thin chains of silver fish
that link and spill and flicker away.

The elements imitate each other:
water-light playing on these stones
becomes a shaking flame; sunlight
stitches the rock-weed's rust and green,
swaying, sea-wavering; one red
twist scatters a shoal like a dust of static
– a million tiny shocks of white
dissolving in the lower depths.
The only sound
is the sea's mouth and the ticking
of the many mouths
that feed within it, sipping the light.

Dreaming high over the sea-forest
– the sea-bed green as a forest floor –
through the columns of gold
and streams of water-weed,
above a world in thrall,

charting by light
as a plane might glide,
slowly, silently
over woods in storm.

ABANDON

That moment, when the sun ignites the valley and picks out
every bud that's greened that afternoon; when birds
spill from the trees like shaken sheets; that sudden loosening
into beauty; the want in her eyes, her eyes' fleet blue;
the medals of light on water; the way the water intrigued
about her feet, the ocean walking her out into its depth,
sea lighting the length of her from the narrow waist
to the weight of the breasts; the way she lifted her eyes to me
and handed me back, simplified; that moment
at the end, knowing the one I had abandoned was myself,
edging with the sun around the bay's scoop of rocks,
rolling the last gold round the glass; that shelving love
as the sun was lost to us and the sky bruised, and the
stones grew cold as the shells on the beach at Naxos.

HAMMERSMITH WINTER

It is so cold tonight; too cold for snow,
and yet it snows. Through the drawn curtain
shines the snowlight I remember as a boy,
sitting up at the window watching it fall.
But you're not here, now, to lead me back
to bed. None of you are. Look at the snow,
I said, to whoever might be near, I'm cold,
would you hold me. Hold me. Let me go.

AT ROANE HEAD

for John Burnside

You'd know her house by the drawn blinds –
by the cormorants pitched on the boundary wall,
the black crosses of their wings hung out to dry.
You'd tell it by the quicken and the pine that hid it
from the sea and from the brief light of the sun,
and by Aonghas the collie, lying at the door
where he died: a rack of bones like a sprung trap.

A fork of barnacle geese came over, with that slow
squeak of rusty saws. The bitter sea's complaining pull
and roll; a whicker of pigeons, lifting in the wood.

She'd had four sons, I knew that well enough,
and each one wrong. All born blind, they say,
slack-jawed and simple, web-footed,
rickety as sticks. Beautiful faces, I'm told,
though blank as air.
Someone saw them once, outside, hirpling
down to the shore, chittering like rats,
and said they were fine swimmers,
but I would have guessed at that.

Her husband left her: said
they couldn't be his, they were more
fish than human,
said they were beglamoured,
and searched their skin for the showing marks.

For years she tended each difficult flame:
their tight, flickering bodies.
Each night she closed
the scales of their eyes to smoor the fire.

Until he came again,
that last time,
thick with drink, saying
he'd had enough of this,
all this witchery,
and made them stand
in a row by their beds,
twitching. Their hands
flapped; herring-eyes
rolled in their heads.
He went along the line
relaxing them
one after another
with a small knife.

It's said she goes out every night to lay
blankets on the graves to keep them warm.
It would put the heart across you, all that grief.

There was an otter worrying in the leaves, a heron
loping slow over the water when I came
at scraich of day, back to her door.

She'd hung four stones in a necklace, wore
four rings on the hand that led me past the room
with four small candles burning

which she called 'the room of rain'.
Milky smoke poured up from the grate
like a waterfall in reverse
and she said my name
and it was the only thing
and the last thing that she said.

She gave me a skylark's egg in a bed of frost;
gave me twists of my four sons' hair; gave me
her husband's head in a wooden box.
Then she gave me the sealskin, and I put it on.

ANNUNCIATION

after Fra Angelico

He has come from the garden, leaving
no shadow, no footprint in the dew.
They hold each other's gaze at the point
of balance: everything streaming
towards this moment, streaming away.

A word will set the seed
of life and death,
the over-shadowing of this girl
by a feathered dark.
But not yet: not quite yet.

How will she remember the silence
of that endless moment?
Or the end, when it all began –
the first of seven joys
before the seven sorrows?

She will remember the aftersong
because she is only human.
One day
she'll wake with wings, or wake
and find them gone.

THE COMING GOD

after Nonnus

Horned child, double-born into risk, guarded
by satyrs, centaurs, raised
by the nymphs of Nysa, by the Hyades:
here he was, the toddler, Dionysus.
He cried 'Daddy!' stretching up to the sky, and he was right
and clever, because the sky *was* Zeus
his father, reaching down.

As he grew, he learnt to flit through other forms;
he'd become a newborn kid, shivering in the corner,
his soft pink skin suddenly the pelt of a goat
and the goat bleating, his hands and feet
now taking their first steps on tottering hooves.

As a grown boy, he would show himself
as a girl, in saffron robes and veils,
moulding his hips
to the coil of a woman's body,
shaping his lips to speak in a woman's voice.

At nine he started to hunt.
He could match the jink
of a coursing hare, reach down at speed
and trip it over; chase alongside a young buck and just
lift it from the running ground
and swing it over his shoulder.

He tamed the wild beasts, just by talking,
and they knelt to be petted, harnessed in.
By his boyhood's end he was dressing in their skins:
the tiger's tree-line stripe, the fallow deer speckled
like a fall of stars,
the pricked ears of the lynx.

One day he came upon a maddened she-bear
and reached out his right hand to her snout
and put his white fingers to her mouth, her teeth,
his fingers gentle at the bristled jaw,
which slackened
and drew in a huge breath
covering the hand of Dionysus with kisses,
wet, coarse, heavy kisses.

A CHILDHOOD

The last bottle of lemonade is nodding
in the rock pool, keeping cold. A childhood,
put away for later. I'm too busy to notice
the sun is going, that they're packing up,
that it's almost time for home. The low waves
warm round my knees as I dig in,
panning for light, happy to be here, dreaming
of the evening I'll wake on the lilo
singing my head off, somewhere
in the sea-lanes to Stavanger, or Oslo.

1964

Under the gritted lid of winter
each ice-puddle's broken plate
cracked to a star. The morning
assembling itself into black and white, the slow dawn
its developing tray. Cold steams off the grass;
the frosted yarrow and sea holly
smoke in the new sun.

*

In the barber-shop mirror, I study this museum of men
through glass: their shaving brushes, talc and whetted razors,
the bottles of bay rum, hair tonic, astringents; long
leather strops; those faded photographs of hairstyles,
that blue Barbicide jar on the counter
dense with pickled combs and scissors like a failed aquarium;
the special drawer full of Durex, copies of *Parade*.

*

The plane from England scores a skater's track
across the icy sky; on the promenade, frost
thistles the railings. You hear the drawl
of the wave, the gulls, raucous at their bins,
the day's first Labrador, his tail flogging the surf.
The quarantined city lies behind, bilge-deep in cobbles,
listing: flying the Yellow Jack, typhoid in its quick-work.

*

On the floor of the butcher's,
blood has rolled through the sawdust
and become round and soft.
We found the blood-buds
in corners as the shop was closing, and gathered
the biggest ones in handkerchiefs to take them
to the woods, break them open for their jelly.

*

In the light from the blaze, there's a fox
nailed to a fence-post: the tricked god
hanging from his wounds. We have nothing to feed
to the fire's many beaks but some mealy apples
and a bottle of Hay's Lemonade, which explodes.
I dig in my pockets and find
a Salvation Army picture of Jesus; tender it to the flame.

*

We'd skip school lunches for some milk,
a rowie and a mutton pie. A twist
of penny sweets: foam bananas, liquorice sticks.
On special days, some hard bonfire toffee
and a lucky bag, watching the third-years fight
in the kirkyard, in among the graves. One boy
holds the other's hair so he can kick him in the face.

*

Creels are swung from boat to shore, filling
fishboxes in silver rows. A slush of ice and gulls
all day till nightfall. Then all you hear is the ice
tightening back together
and the cats crying that dreadful way they have,
like the sound of babies singing
lullabies to other babies.

*

I knew how children came, so I look for the stork
in the cliffs over the mussel pools,
in the quarry ledges, the chimney stacks,
all along the walking pylons –
search for her everywhere
in the gantries of the storm woods, in the black pines,
that she might take me back.

UNDER BEINN RUADHAINN

for Andrew O'Hagan

Three moons in the sky
the night they found him
drowned in Sawtan's Bog;
just his cap, sitting there
and his wee fat hands poking out.

It was no loss to the village,
I told them next morning,
and the villagers agreed.
Horn-daft, he was,
havering and glaikit
and scaring the children.

I mind that time
he picked up a mouse and ate it, quick,
in two mouthfuls;
set the tail aside
on the ground
like a cocktail stick.

I used her well, after that,
his Jennie,
still in her widow's weeds,
jilping into her
whenever I could,
in the barn or the boat-house
or off in the fields.
She slipped two or three out at least,
and sank each one in a lobster creel.

Her head was away
by the end, as mad as her man
and no good to me.
She sleeps now
under Beinn Ruadhainn, her face
covered in ivy,
scab, and sticky-willow.

Then the dreams came.
Last night: the burning loch,
so full of bairns
they bobbed to the surface
with their hair on fire;
black snow; rain
like razorblades;
the foosty-faced man,
there at every corner,
hands furred with grey-mould.
And her, as always,
star-naked, hatching
in the herring-nets.
The last I remember was my body
being driven with sticks through the town
to Sawtan's Brae, and hanged.

I broke from sleep and sat up in the dark.
I groped around for the matches
and the matches were put in my hand.

CORRYVRECKAN

'a depe horlepoole quhairin if schippis do enter thair is no refuge
but death onlie'
Alexander Lindsay, *A Rutter of the Scottish Seas*, c. 1540

Thickening in these narrows to some height and speed,
squeezing through the Great Door, Dorus Mhor,
the sea's so high it's climbing over itself to get through.
They call these 'the overfalls'. A sluice through a bottleneck.
A great seething. The frenzy of water feeding on water.

Seen from above, the tidal race is a long army moving fast
across a plain as flat and grey as a shield of polished steel,
to reach, at the end, the terrible turbulence of battle.
A blue stream turned to a gutter of broken water:
water that's stood its ground, churning; sea
kept back and held in standing waves:
walls of water, each as tall as a church door,
endlessly breaking on the same point –
each wave swallowing its own form
and returning, re-making itself, chained there
on its own wheel, turning black to white to black.

The sea gets stranger beyond the sentry waves –
a round of slow slack-water, barely moving,
ringed by raging white: a close,
oily calm, unnaturally smooth, like a metal blank.
Then you see them – these
errors on the still surface – sudden
disturbances, boils that bulge and blister, burst,
small holes that appear, whirling open
as if a hundred sink-plugs had been pulled.

Then the huge round rises up: dead-level, streaming,
upwelling, holding its shape like some giant plate
that's been lying just under the water
being lifted up fast and then
dropped back down, the sea
sucking in after it,
from all sides, into its absence, waves
shearing over, folding in to the core, the depth
and the great black gullet of loss.
The maelstrom. The long throat of Corryvreckan.
The opened body of water that today we rode across.

A QUICK DEATH

'It is not.'
Samuel Beckett

Blue-shelled, blue-blooded,
with eight legs, two
stalked eyes and a toothed stomach.
Heraldic: *azure, attired,*
armed at all points, in pride.

At rest, a blue-black gauntlet;
at war, a clacking samurai in lacquered plates, a fighter
swaying with his huge gloves, leading
with the smaller claw – the pincher, the seizer –
holding back the crusher, letting it drag.

The face, a tool-chest, a cutler's dream,
five sets of exterior mouthparts, a team of blades
moving constantly; the fantail skirt
splays open, the swimmerets
scissoring underneath.

*

The three ante-rooms of death: the creel's
'kitchen' and 'parlour', and this restaurant tank
which we might as well call 'the larder'. The lobster
shuffles across its floor and taps the glass
twice, claws muffled by rubber bands.

The forecast is for stormy weather. Read it
in the glass, my fine dark handsome stranger;
it's the same for us all in the end –
a short journey: eyes first
into the fire.

DIONYSUS IN LOVE

after Nonnus

Hardened by the hills of Phrygia,
quickened by its streams, the boy-god
Dionysus came of age.

And as his own body changed
his eyes grew wider, and turned
towards the bodies of others.
Ampelos was the one, above all:
most beautiful boy, most beautiful
of satyrs: lean and long and new.
Even his flaws were gorgeous:
the bony nubs at the forehead, that slight
skip in his step, sometimes;
the way he slept in a curve, his soft tail
slacked over his haunches.

Dionysus let him win at wrestling: flesh
on flesh, their knotted hands, legs
pressed against legs.
Then to feel those muscles of his
tighten in the flank
and flip him over,
so he could lie still under that weight.

Dionysus held back at the sprint,
to watch: the god
of spark and springheel, the god

who would cross continents with a single step
stood still, and with one breath
blew speed into his love's young body,
lifting it over the line.

Their race in the red river was the last test,
and glowing Ampelos matched it, red for red,
his colour rising as he met it,
rose to rose, and swept past Dionysus
who had watched him
from the corner of his eye,
and slowed.

The boy hoisted himself up from the river
streaming in victory, and went to the forest
where he gathered vipers to bind in his hair,
killed a deer for its dappled skin,
and leapt on the back of a mountain bear
and rode him out of the wood, all in imitation
of the god Dionysus.

Who stood, watching Ampelos.
Then drew him close, with a warning,
saying the boy need not fear
the sharp mouths of panthers, lions or bears,
only dread the horns of beasts –
for he had seen a horned dragon
rise from the rocks
with a fawn on its back
which it tossed down onto the stone altar,
gored it through

and feasted.
He had seen the blood fork
over the rocks into pools, pools
that filled and fell again
like some long dark drink
that spilled out thickly, slug
after slug, till it slowed
and dripped to a stop.

Dionysus watched him; never tired of watching,
though fearful now, for what he had seen.

And Ampelos watched him back,
every day, Dionysus
riding away on the saddle of a panther
to hunt the dark woods
with his maenads, with his deer-skin
whipping behind him,
out on the hunt
like a god.

And as he watched, he felt a presence
at his shoulder saying
'Why should *he* have the panthers,
why should *he* be the grand one?
Why don't you ride at his side
on the back of a bull, to please
the bull-king, for him to see you
with a bull between your knees?
The girl Europa
rode one bareback over our great sea

with no reins or bridle;
surely you can take a bull
and master it –
surely you can ride the forest?'
And as he turned
there was no one there.

And then the forest parted, and there it stood:
the bull, its huge mouth slopped open,
a grey tongue thick as the boy's arm
hung out in a curl
like some third horn
as it lowered its head to the running stream
and drank.
And as it drank, Ampelos pulled up rushes,
plaiting some into a bridle,
twisting others round an alder stem
to make a kind of whip.
Then he gathered lilies and anemones,
hyacinths and roses from the river bank
and strung them through, in a garland.
The bull stood, patiently,
and bent its head for the boy,
who stroked its brow, felt
the hard weight of its horns –
horns he dressed in flowers to the tips –
before he swung up on the bull's back,
slipped on the bridle, and called out
to Selene, goddess of the horned moon,
gleaming bull-driver in the night sky,
shouting 'Look! I am riding the horned bull!'

And the sky-goddess looked down
at this satyr, and sent him a reward
for his insolence: a gadfly –
goad and tormentor of beasts.
With the first sting the bull lurched forward
into a run, the second driving it wild
and away from the river up through the rocks,
maddened into a gallop, the boy
hanging on, the beast plunging higher
into the mountains,
trying to shake off the stinging fly.
In its frenzy the bull
bucked so hard
it threw the boy headlong over its back
and there was a small crack
like the snap of a twig, and the bull
stood over the broken boy
and ran him through with its horns.

Dionysus found the white body lying
in its great red star,
laid anemones on his dead love's open eyes
and a fawn-skin over him to keep
his stopped heart from the cold.
He stood by the boy, watching the red
tendrils branch and twine through the rocks,
and being a god he could not weep
for Ampelos – could neither grieve, nor follow him
down to the land of the dead.

Then Dionysus heard a voice that said,
'Free this love for another, and forget.
When a flower dies, the gardener
must learn to plant again.'

And Dionysus, who never wept,
wept then for Ampelos,
and his tears fell on the boy
and the boy's body started to change.
His feet taking root and the long legs
thickening to stems, his belly twisting
into a stalk that broke into branches
and he shot up his own shape:
leaves grew from his fingers, and up
from the buds of his horns
burst clusters of grapes, hard and green.

Dionysus stood under the vine
that had been Ampelos, and it ripened for him.
He drew some fruit from the stem
like a woman would pull off earrings
and he squeezed them in his fist
till his wrist was laced with red.
Then he licked it, and said: 'You are still alive,
sweet friend, even if you are gone.
You have kept your rosy colour
and you taste of heaven.
I will wear your leaves in my hair instead of snakes
and wind your young shoots round my fennel wand.
I will let you soak through me.'

And so, wine was made,
and we made from it: abandon, delirium,
a cure for regret, an end to love and grief.
We hold it in our hands: a brief forgetting.

THE FISHERMEN'S FAREWELL

Their long stares mark them apart; eyes gone
to sea-colours: grey, foam-flecked

and black in the undertow, blue
as the blue banners of the mackerel, whipping west.

On land, they are smoke-walkers, where each stone
is a standing stone, every circle a stone circle.

They would be rumour if they could, in this frozen
landscape like a stopped sea, from the great stone keels

of Callanish to the walls of Dunnottar and Drum.
They would be less even than rumour:

to be ocean-stealers, to never throw a shadow –
to dream the blank horizon and dread the sight of land.

The drink storms through these men, uncompasses
them, till they're all at sea again.

Their houses, heeled over in the sand:
each ruin now a cairn for kites.

And down by the quay
past empty pots, unmended nets and boats:

this tiny bar, where men sleep upright
in their own element, as seals.

THE HALVING

(Royal Brompton Hospital, 1986)

General anaesthesia; a median sternotomy
achieved by sternal saw; the ribs
held aghast by retractor; the tubes
and cannulae drawing the blood
to the reservoir, and its bubbler;
the struggling aorta
cross-clamped, the heart
chilled and stopped and left to dry.
The incompetent bicuspid valve excised,
the new one – a carbon-coated disc, housed
expensively in a cage of tantalum –
is broken from its sterile pouch
then heavily implanted into the native heart,
bolstered, seated with sutures.
The aorta freed, the heart re-started.
The blood allowed back
after its time abroad
circulating in the machine.
The rib-spreader relaxed
and the plumbing removed, the breast-bone
lashed with sternal wires, the incision closed.

Four hours I'd been away: out of my body.
Made to die then jerked back to the world.
The distractions of delirium
came and went and then,
as the morphine drained, I was left with a split

chest that ground and grated on itself.
Over the pain, a blackness rose and swelled;
'pump-head' is what some call it
– debris from the bypass machine
migrating to the brain – but it felt
more interesting than that.
Halved and unhelmed,
I have been away, I said to the ceiling,
and now I am not myself.

THE GHOST OF ACTAEON

'You are sleeping, Mother, and do not know my fate.
I wish you could wake and embrace me, much changed
as I am with the horns and the hair of a stag
and only the eyes and voice the same as Actaeon.
My dogs did what I'd trained them to do: forgive them.
If you see my lost bow, break it: bury it with my bones.
I know you found no sign of them in the woods,
but look again. Look for a freckled coat and not a tunic,
branched antlers not smooth temples, and longer legs
than you remember, that end not in feet, but in hooves.'

A & E

It was like wetting the bed
waking up that night, soaked through:
my sutures open again
and the chest wound haemorrhaging.
Pulling on jeans and an overcoat
I called a car to Camberwell, and
in through the shivering rubber doors
presented myself
at that Saturday-night abattoir
of Casualty at King's on Denmark Hill.

At this front-line, behind her desk
and barred window, the triage nurse
was already waving me away –
till I parted the tweed to show her
what I had going on underneath.
Unfashionable, but striking nonetheless:
my chest undone like some rare waistcoat,
with that lace-up front – a black *échelle* –
its red, wet-look leatherette,
those fancy, flapping lapels.

FALCONER'S FAREWELL

She kept a cast of merlins
mewed in her own chamber; let him
fletch his shafts with each new
throw of feathers.

He strung his bow with sinew, the very nerve
of a deer, so he'd draw with such speed and gift
he could pin a pair of arrows
on the head of a man, like horns.

When she heard the lark ringing up high
over September, she slipped herself free;
her blue hunger reading the sky – the land
already dropping under her.

His flights missed their mark, slid on the hard,
dry ground, snaked into the grass.
When he looked for them he felt them, snapping
underfoot. And her, nowhere to be found.

STRINDBERG IN SKOVLYST

I.

A manor house in ruin. It suits me down to the ground.
A tower to write in,
three rooms for the family, with a kitchen,
and all for fifty crowns a month.
Unbelievably filthy, I have to say: everything
broken, unfinished, abandoned.
In the yard, two floors below, a mongrel
half-heartedly mounts a greyhound; blue flies
are hatching in the dung. It fits my mood.
Wherever you look: neglect, failure,
all the shit you could wish for.
A home away from home.

They laid on quite a show, trying to get us to take the place:
goblets of flaming spirits, the Countess
with a hurdy-gurdy, lying on the floor;
her steward as circus-master, conjurer,
with his not-so-beautiful assistant,
the blonde fat girl in a spangled costume.
All the usual card tricks, which I knew,
but then he got her up to the ceiling on poles, then
whipped them away – and she stayed there,
in the air, levitating above us. And she didn't fall.

I gave them three months' rent after that, up front.

II.

The Countess is mad – today and every day –
quite mad, and this is her menagerie;
the cattle and horses stay outside, eating thatch,
but the rest are residents: cats, poultry, eight huge dogs.
She carries a white lamb, sometimes,
but her favourite is Sky-Leaper, the blind,
ancient cockerel she dandles on her lap.
Like magic, rabbits hop out of coal-scuttles,
turkeys squabble in the bath-tub, eating soap.
With a flourish, she reveals
a litter of white kittens in a drawer
then, shyly, from the front of the sky-blue
off-the-shoulder dress she wears each day,
she pulls a duckling.
A pigeon flies through the window,
followed by the male, who ambles after her,
his lady-love: blowing his crop, dragging
his spread tail through the dirt.
An unearthly screech, then the stately
step of an Indian peacock, rustling down the corridor
towards the room
where two Great Danes are standing
six-legged on the shaky bed, coupling.
Speaking of which, here's Hansen,
her steward (and more than *that*, I suspect):
a black-fingered trickster with his
wagging forelock and dice for eyes,
up and about, flaunting
his yellow suit, the peacock feather in his hat.

And behind him, the maid – who I take
for his sister – Martha Magdalene:
sixteen if she's a day, blonde *knullhår*,
barely decent with her predatory mouth
and her dress a size too small.

A three-hander, then, with this shambles for a stage:
this home to pestilence, cluster flies, blowflies, men
and women, Ragnarök, Armageddon –
my crucible will turn this all to gold.
In my head, when the gales are riding wild,
I steer towards catastrophe
then write about it.

III.

*Interior. The upper rooms. Noise of children. Dim summer sunlight
through the grimy, curtainless windows. The playwright's wife is
boiling sheets, swabbing the floorboards with bleach.*

*Interior. Kitchen. The walls and ceilings black with soot, the tables
piled with unwashed dishes, rotting food. A side of mutton hangs
from a hook on the wall, just high enough to be out of reach of the dogs.
The maid, Martha, is shelling peas.*

*Exterior. The pavilion on the lake. The steward, Hansen, and the
playwright in animated conversation, drinking schnapps.*

I confess, with a clink of glasses, to six months' celibacy
at the hand of Artemis, my wife,
but he doesn't understand.

That I hate women but desire them –
hate them *because* I desire them.
The power they have.
That I fear I might go mad.
That I am, already, mad.
He sighs, and tells me his ridiculous stories,
shows me conjuring tricks,
sings the same song over and over again.
I only listen when he shares his hopes
for advancement – the dream of climbing
to the top of the high tree
to rob the nest of its golden egg –
but how the trunk is too smooth to gain purchase,
and the branches too high to catch hold.

Exterior. Garden. The Countess and the playwright walking between
the vegetable plots, overgrown with burdock and nettles, cobbled with
turds.

She was going on about her animals, her *family*,
and I thought of that pack of feral dogs –
vile scavengers – and all the rest:
all the tettered, emaciated beasts.
She said she dreamt she was on top of a high pillar
and all she wanted was to fall.

Interior. The tower room. Midnight.

The girl, at my door again. What was I to do
against those lead-grey eyes, the tousled hair,
that young, thick body? That *mouth*?
The bestial ruin stinking in my face.

The snort and rut coming closer.
I ran my thumb down the seam,
opening up the velvet
to touch the hard pod of the bean.
She kissed me like a cat.
Cats kill you at the throat, so I was quickly
over her, and in. Behind the trees
a filament of lightning briefly glowed
and died. Manumission.
And now: the fall.

IV.

The voices in my head are company at last
in these high rooms
in the glove of the night, under a fretted moon.
That gypsy Hansen's out there drunk with a gun
shouting about 'corrupting a minor' and
'raping my sister'. Letting off shots.
I was on her *once*
and all I got out of it was scabies, and now infamy.
I told the Countess that her lover's
just a common thief;
she said, 'My brother, you mean.'

Our bags are packed.
The carriage waits below.
I have stoked the fever enough to spark some fire.
It's dreadful, I tell myself, but there's no other way.
We are above such people.
But now it's done. And now I have my play.

THE CAVE OF SLEEP

after Ovid

Deep inside a hollow mountain there's a cave
where the sun's rays never reach;
the earth around it
breathes out
clouds of fog
into this endless twilight,
this secret dwelling-place
of the god of idle Sleep.
There is no cockerel to summon the dawn,
no geese, no dogs, no beasts of any kind
to break the silence, not even branches
stirring in the breeze. Only stillness here,
and the distant murmur far below
of the River Lethe moving pebbles
as it goes, whispering *sleep, sleep*.
Huge lush poppies stand in rows outside;
herbs steep their juices in the night,
infusing the ground with a slow release,
a mulled gravity.
There are no doors, in case a turning hinge
might creak, and no guardian at the gate.
On a platform in the middle of the cave
is a bed of ebony
thick with dark linens, soft black pillows,
where the god himself
lies, deeply, languidly, at peace.
Around him, on all sides, are empty dreams,

countless as ears of corn
at harvest-time, leaves on the forest trees
or grains of sand along the shore.

The messenger of the goddess enters the chamber,
brushing aside the dreams that stand in her way.
The brightness of her robes begins to fill the cave
and Sleep starts to stir, struggling
to lift his eyelids, heavy in slumber.
Over and over again he tries, then falls back,
head sinking into his chest. At last
he wakes, blinks open his eyes and
hoisting himself up on one elbow,
looks at the woman and smiles.

DIONYSUS AND THE MAIDEN

after Nonnus

I

Her only home was here in this forest, among the high rocks,
sending her long arrows in flight through the standing pines
as if threading nets in the air.
She'd never seen a cup of wine or a perfumed room, or a bed:
she drank chill water from the mountain brook and had only ever
lain with lionesses, newly delivered of their cubs, who licked
her hard white body, whimpering there like dogs.

She was not alone in the woods: the breeze shook her hair, lifted
the edge of her tunic on those bare legs
as she ran on the rocks, climbing
after a huge stag, and stopped; felt for the shaft
and quickly nocked it to the bowstring, drew, and let it loose.

She was not alone: a young shepherd was watching,
trying to call up the breeze to lift her again. He wanted to be
her quiver, her spear, and when he found all her weapons in a cave
he was swept with such longing he kissed her coiled nets
and pressed an arrow to his lips – which is how she found him.

'Save me from this passion, this fire that feeds under my heart!
If you can never love me, as you must know now that I love you,
then to watch your bow-arm tighten and your breast rise and steady
is all I can ever ask, so fix me in the heart to end this hurt . . .'

Despite her shaking fury, her disgust, she drew fast and clean:
pinning the last words back in with his tongue,
filling his mouth with feathers.

II

He was done now with satyrs, took no pleasure in his Bacchae.
Dionysus – he whose colours were never true – had seen her
swimming naked in a pool, seen her again in the flowers:
arms of lily-white, cheeks of the rose, eyes of hyacinth blue.

'If you wish for a chamber in the forest,' he said, 'I will grow
grapevine round a glade strewn with ferns and petals of iris,
and lay a piled bed of dappled fawn-skins there
for you, to rest your head on the shoulder of Dionysus.'

'Touch me or my bow or quiver and you'll follow
that lovesick shepherd . . . Believe me, I will wound
the unwoundable Dionysus. I refuse your bed,
your perfumed hair, your woman's body, even if it's true
your veins beat with the blood of Zeus.
I'll take no man for a lord, and no god either.'
And with that she went plunging into the forest.

For days he tracked her, kept her on high ground
away from the water; let the thirst for it draw her back down.
He opened his arms and darkened the river with wine;
folded his arms, and she drank it down in draughts.
Her world doubled. She turned her eyes round
to the wide yawning lake, and she saw two lakes;

the hills swung around her as her head grew heavy
and her feet slipped under her, under the heavy wing
of sleep, and deep into this: her wedding slumber.

He came to her then, undid the end of the knot, releasing
a teeming fragrance of flowers, and ivy, and vine
with grapes in its leaves as a screen for the bed,
for the stolen bridal, for the pleasure of Dionysus.
He entered her the way light breaks through mountains;
gave her this: his gift of going,
made the noise of a cliff, and fell away.

She woke in her pain to a bed of skins and leaves, her thighs
soaked through. She wept and raged at her abandonment by the gods.
All the gods but one.
She thought to set a sword to her throat, cast herself
rolling off some crag; to cut apart the river where she drank,
burn down the mountains, uproot the forest where she ran.
But it was him she wanted most: to track him and find him and drain
his heart's blood on her dagger's blade. Take his breath away.
She wandered the high hills for weeks, months, into winter,
casting her nets at shadows, pitching her lance at the dark.
With every sound she heard, she freed flocks of arrows into the air,
into the body of the god, she hoped.
But Dionysus *was* air, and she was alone in the woods,
following these tracks
of a beast, or a man, or a god
when they were just her own tracks in the snow.

THE SHELTER

I should never have stayed here
in this cold shieling
once the storm passed
and the rain had finally eased.

I could make out shapes
inside, the occasional sound:
a muffled crying
which I took for wind in the trees;
a wasp,
stuttering there at the windowsill.
I listened. What looked like
a small red coat
was dripping from its wire hanger.

There was a shift and rustle
coming from the bucket in the corner
by the door; I found, inside,
a crumpled fist of balled-up paper, slowly
uncrinkling.

On the hearth, just legible
in the warm ash, my name and dates,
and above that, in a shard
of mirror left in the frame,
I caught sight of myself, wearing
something like a black brooch at the neck.
Then I looked more closely
and saw what it was.

PARTYTIME

You were quite the vision last night
I remember, before my vision went.

And I was left,
instead,
with this
falling corridor of edges,
the greased slipway
and its black drop: that
glint of fracture
in the faces, in the disco-ball's
pellets of light,
in the long whiskies I threw back
short and hard.
Streeling I was, and streeling I went
through some heavy gate
I came across –
and left the world on the other side, the dark
slowly calving over me
on the white slope,
on the sledge of night.

You liked my sensitive hands, you said,
but my hands are empty.
I will give you everything
but have nothing to give.

And now: now
I'll fall back

on instinct, compass,
the ghost in the sleeve,
find my way home to a place
so small I can barely stand.
The city has flooded, emptied,
flooded again.
I don't know where I am.
Your door is near, someone laughed,
just around that corner.
The frightened boy
climbed out of me and ran.

PUNCHINELLO'S FAREWELL

after Tiepolo

Straightening up his sugarloaf hat, he stoops
– all thumbs, fumbling the buttons –
and drops his trousers: staring, blankly,
at these marbled thighs, grey
knees, the mealy, withered shanks.
Lifting the dense lard of his belly, he
spots what he thought he was missing
– his butcher's apostrophe –
and does a little shuffling dance,
half-masted, with a chalky grin.

He'd woken with a spark in his throat
and they'd been at it all morning,
guzzling jug after jug of Valpolicella,
mopping it up with gnocchi.
Made a scene in town with their yells and jokes,
their somersaults and tumbling, crowing
like roosters and gaping at girls:
crowding round them, flicking their skirts,
sniffing below for that soppy smell, that
briny, cowrie-shell tang.

His pal, still holding the neck of a bottle,
is blotto: out cold in the *mezzogiorno* heat.
Hobbling over to a broken bench he squats,
finds the right position and, sheepish,
sniggering, lets out a sludge of wine and macaroni.

He will be gone, soon enough,
when the light turns aubergine,
but a hundred more of him will take his place,
with their conical hats, white suits, thirsts
and hungers, their humpbacks and their beaks.

THE HOUSE OF RUMOUR

after Ovid

At the world's centre
between earth and sky and sea
is a place where every sound can be heard,
where everything is seen.
Here Rumour lives,
making her home on a mountain-top.
This house stands open
night and day: a dome
of apertures and windows set
like a million eyes at gaze,
steady, unblinking,
no doors or shutters anywhere.
Her walls have ears.
They *are* ears. The whole house
made from thinly-beaten,
resonating bronze, hums
constantly
with words repeating back to themselves
round and round, again
and again: the low susurration
of echoing sound.
No silence anywhere,
just the murmur of voices
like whispering waves
or the last low rolling crush of thunder.
The house is haunted by shadows,
ghosts that come and go, a host of rumours,

the false mixed with the true,
words and phrases, fact, fictions,
fabrications, all confused.
At every turn, a story spreads
and grows and changes, each new teller
adding on to what they've heard.
Here is surveillance, interception;
a multitude of recording angels.
Here lives rash Credulity, reckless Error,
groundless Joy. Whispers
make their home here, alongside
sudden Sedition, tremulous Fear.
Rumour herself
hears everything, sees
everything that happens in the heavens,
in the sea or on the earth;
invigilator, sentinel, echo-chamber,
she misses nothing
misses no one as she sweeps the world.

THE GOD WHO DISAPPEARS

after Nonnus

Born to a life of dying, the boy-god's first death came
when he could barely crawl, the budding horns just there,
nudged among curls, as he played on the floor
with his toys: a knuckle-bone, ball and spinning-top,
golden apples, a tuft of wool, and
on his other side, the thunderbolts of Zeus.

They entered the throne-room's dark,
their round faces smeared with chalk into pale moons,
and they slid forward, drawing their hungry knives.
He saw them in the mirror, looming behind him
in a hundred reflections,
and he watched his body swim through other shapes:
a doubled-up ancient with a face of rain,
a blank-eyed baby, downy youth. Then he saw the mane
of a lion, jaws opening, the sinewed neck
of a bridling horse, the darting tongue
and poison fangs and coils stretching
for the throat of one of the murderers, then
twisting, to the leap of a tiger, the shouldering,
heavy-horned bull, and then suddenly the great bull
shuddered to a stop,
and they started slicing him
to piecemeal; so many blades
he could see in the mirror,
working on the bull-shaped Dionysus.
He followed his image into the glass, and was soon

split and scattered, divided up, diced
into the universe.

*

He spends his life dying. The god who comes,
the god who disappears. Dismembered,
he is resurrected. He is beside us; beside himself.
Ghost of abandon, and abandoning,
he shatters us to make us whole.

FINDING THE KEYS

The set seed and the first bulbs showing.
The silence that brings the deer.

The trees are full of handles and hinges;
you can make out keyholes, latches in the leaves.

Buds tick and crack in the sun, break open
slowly in a spur of green.

*

The small-change colours of the river bed:
these stones of copper, silver, gold.

The rock-rose in the waste-ground
finding some way to bloom. The long

spill of birdsong. Flowers, all
turned to face the hot sky. Nothing stirs.

*

That woody clack of antlers.
In yellow and red, the many griefs of autumn.

The dawn light through amber leaves
and the trees are lanterned, blown

the next day to empty stars.
Smoke in the air; the air, turning.

*

Under a sky of stone and pink
faring in from the north and promising snow:

the blackbird.
In his beak, a victory of worms.

The winged seed of the maple,
the lost keys under the ash.

CRIMOND

i.m. Jessie Seymour Irvine

Daughter of the manse of Dunnottar, then Peterhead
and Crimond, all north-eastern edges over unstill waters,
what softness brought this tune from your young hands?
The tune my father called for every Sunday: the 23rd psalm.
When I hear it now, it's all wet cobbles and the haar
rolling in down the street outside, and him
shaking their hands, sharp in his black and white:
the dog-collar (I knew) cut clean from a bottle of Fairy Liquid.
How far we all are from where we thought we'd be:
those parishioners all vanished long ago; my father – ash
above the crematorium; me, swimming back-crawl
through the valley of the shadow of death, and you –
not even a photograph left of you – the girl who will never
touch again the foot of the cross at Crimond.

GLASS OF WATER AND COFFEE POT

after Chardin

These rooms of wood, of tongue-and-groove, open out
on a garden of white-washed walls and a maple tree,
a new Spring bright among the weathered stone and brick.
We find things that are old and used, well-made, well worn
and beautiful because of this. The balance
intimate between that glass of water's clarity and light
and the pot's grave darkness: an order so luminous
and fine you needn't measure it with a rule, just look.
The papery whiteness of the garlic heads is the same light
held in the water glass, the same light lifting a gleam
from the blackened coffee pot that's somehow managed
to make it through, to find harmony here
on this stone shelf, happiness of the hand and heart,
to keep its heat and still pour clean and true.

PORT NA H-ABHAINNE

We walked the cliff of Portnahaven
listening to the grey seals sing
on Orsay and Eilean Mhic Coinnich
across the little harbour.

Were they singing for the love
of being here in this place, like us,
far from griefs – and were they also
singing, as we were, to each other?

THE KEY

The door
to the walled garden, the place
I'd never been,
was opened

with a simple turn
of the key
I'd carried with me
all these years.

Notes & Acknowledgements

The Flaying of Marsyas
from *Metamorphoses*, Book VI

shirt-lifting: the common name for the mujahideen practice, in Afghanistan in the 1980s, of stripping the skin from the backs of Russian prisoners

Hands of a Farmer in Co. Tyrone
sheugh: (*Scots*) a ditch or trough

The Flowers of the Forest
A lament for the battle of Flodden, thought to bring bad luck to the piper who plays it, unless he introduces a deliberate error in his delivery. This poem and the 'Six Views' that follow are from 'Camera Obscura' – a sequence of poems built on the personal and artistic life of David Octavius Hill, the pioneering Edinburgh photographer.

The Language of Birds
a pigeon's heart . . . stuck through with pins: a charm sometimes used by lovesick or vengeful girls to summon or afflict their faithless lovers

swans go singing out to sea: one of the more familiar legends about swans is that they sing before they die; Aristotle suggests that when they sense the approach of death the birds fly out to sea

Maroon, Over Black on Red
Mark Rothko (1903–1970)

The Long Home
the long home: the grave

Asterion and the God

Asterion: the given name of the Minotaur, half-brother to Ariadne – the princess who betrayed the god Dionysus for the hero, Theseus

nec enim praesentior illo est deus: as Acoetes says of Dionysus in Ovid's *Metamorphoses* (III, 658–9): 'no god is nearer than him'

Fall

Rilke wrote 'Herbst' ('Autumn') soon after arriving in Paris in 1902, on 11 September

The Death of Actaeon

from *Metamorphoses*, Book III

Selkie

selkie: in Celtic legend, selkies are shape-changers with the ability to live in two elements; they swim as seals in the water but can cast off their pelts on land and assume human form

bodhrán: (Irish) a traditional Irish drum; pronounced *bough-rawn*

Actaeon: the Early Years

pleitered: (Scots) dabbled aimlessly with the hands and feet

lucken toes: (Scots) toes joined by a web of skin; those born with this condition were sometimes known as *Sliocha nan Ron*, the Children of the Seal

La Stanza delle Mosche

La Stanza delle Mosche: (Italian) The Room of Flies

Holding Proteus

In Book IV of the *Odyssey*, Menelaus, King of Sparta, recalls being becalmed under the spell of the gods on the island of Pharos. The only way he can escape is with the help of Proteus, the Old Man of the Sea: a shape-shifting prophet who so dislikes being questioned that he will assume any form to avoid his questioners. Menelaus captures the god, holding him tight as he changes successively into a variety of animal, vegetable and elemental forms before returning to the human. Proteus is then obliged to break the binding spell and free the waters.

Signs on a White Field

sun-cups: hollows in ice caused by surface melting during intense sunshine

snow penitents: pinnacles or spikes of compacted snow or ice caused by partial ablation of an ice field exposed to the sun

By Clachan Bridge

stone-baby: the medical term is *lithopedion*; this occurs when a foetus dies during an ectopic pregnancy, is too large to be reabsorbed by the body, and calcifies

The Plague Year

observatory: the Griffith Observatory in Los Angeles was the scene of the knife fight in 'Rebel Without a Cause' (1955)

Pere Marquette: pronounced *peer*

A Gift

dwayberries: deadly nightshade – a poison, as are all the plants mentioned

Strindberg in Berlin

Strindberg took a flat in Berlin in the autumn of 1892 and became a regular at *Zum Schwarzen Ferkel*, where he first encountered Munch, Hamsun and the Polish writer and musician Stanisław Przybyszewski. During his brief stay in the city he met, and became engaged to, Frida Uhl, while conducting an affair with the young Norwegian, Dagny Juel. Strindberg and Munch were rivals for Juel's attentions, but she married Przybyszewski. It was around this time that Strindberg's lifelong interest in alchemy began.

mareld: (Swedish) sea-fire, also known in English as 'seasparkle': the phenomenon of bioluminescence, where high concentrations of plankton (*Noctiluca scintillans*) containing an enzyme called luciferas give off light when disturbed

Leaving St Kilda

This describes an anti-clockwise circumnavigation of the main island, Hirta, then Soay, followed by a clockwise turn around Boreray

Tinsel

tinsel: the losing of something, or the sustaining of harm, damage, or detriment; loss

Widow's Walk

the widow's walk: a high coastal walk or platform where fishermen's wives waited for sight of the returning boats

At Roane Head

quicken: the rowan

Annunciation

The fresco 'The Annunciation' by Fra Angelico in Museo Nazionale di San Marco in Florence

The Coming God

from *Dionysiaca*, Books IX, XIV

1964

The year of the typhoid epidemic in Aberdeen

Under Beinn Ruadhainn

Beinn Ruadhainn: (Gaelic) 'summit of the red place'; 'Ruadhainn' anglicised as 'Ruthven', pronounced *riven*

horn-daft: quite mad

havering: babbling, speaking nonsense

glaikit: vacant, idiotic

jilping: spurting, spilling

foosty: mouldy, gone bad

Corryvreckan

The third biggest whirlpool in the world; to be found between Jura and Scarba

Dionysus in Love

from *Dionysiaca*, Books X, XI, XII

Falconer's Farewell

mewed: put a hawk in a quiet place to moult

Strindberg in Skovlyst

In the summer of 1888, Strindberg rented rooms with his wife, Siri von Essen, and their children, in the manor house at Skovlyst, near Copenhagen. The marriage had collapsed but the family was still travelling together around Europe. In exile, Strindberg had recently fallen heavily under the influence of the writings of Nietzsche. During the summer in Skovlyst, he wrote – amongst other things – his most famous play, *Miss Julie*.

The poem incorporates images from *Miss Julie* and some adapted original lines: two from the play and one from a contemporary letter from Strindberg to Verner von Heidenstam.

knullhår: (Swedish) pronounced *knool-hoer*: a neologism, literally 'fuck-hair', suggestive of dishevelled, post-coital tangles

The Cave of Sleep

from *Metamorphoses*, Book XI

Dionysus and the Maiden

from *Dionysiaca*, Books XV, XVI

Punchinello's Farewell

The drawing by Giovanni Battista Tiepolo notionally titled '*Due Pulcinella, uno disteso e l'altro seduto*' ('Two Punchinellos, one stretched

out and the other seated') in the Fondazione Giorgio Cini, San Giorgio
Maggiore, Venice

The House of Rumour

from *Metamorphoses*, Book XII

The God Who Disappears

from *Dionysiaca*, Book VI

Crimond

Jessie Seymour Irvine (1836–87) was the daughter of Alexander Irvine,
a Church of Scotland minister. She wrote the tune 'Crimond' in her
teens, and it is now the standard setting for the 23rd psalm.

Glass of Water and Coffee Pot

The painting by Jean-Baptiste-Siméon Chardin, in the Carnegie
Museum of Art, Pittsburgh

Port na h-Abhainne

Port na h-Abhainne: (Gaelic) 'harbour at the river'; a village in the
south-west of Islay, anglicised as Portnahaven, pronounced
port na haa-vin

*

I am grateful to all the editors: Barbara Epstein, Jonathan Galassi,
Michael Hofmann, John Lanchester, James Lasdun, Jean McNicol,
Andrew O'Hagan, Don Paterson, Bob Silvers, Peter Straus and
Drenka Willen.